AN ALLE COOKBOOK

RECIPES FREE FROM EGGS, MILK, CHEESE, BUTTER, WHEAT FLOUR, CHOCOLATE, SALT, SUGAR, BAKING POWDER AND CORNFLOUR

Vegetarian edition

Patricia Carter

IAN HENRY PUBLICATIONS, Ltd.
PLAYERS PRESS, Inc.

© copyright, J P Carter, 1981, 1989, 1993

First edition, 1981
Third (vegetarian) edition, 1993

British Library Cataloguing in Publication Data

Carter, Patricia
An allergy cookbook. - 3rd ed.
1. Food allergic persons. Food - Recipes
I. Title
641.5'63

ISBN 0-86025-450-X
0-88734 629 4 [U.S.A.]

Published simultaneously
in the United Kingdom by
Ian Henry Publications, Ltd.,
20 Park Drive, Romford, Essex RM1 4LH
and in the United States of America by
Players Press, Inc.
P.O.Box 1132, Studio City, California 91614-0132
Printed by
Redwood Books
Kennet House, Kennet Way
Trowbridge, Wiltshire BA14 8RN

CONTENTS

Listed below are a number of American suppliers, which may be useful for obtaining replacement products for local people.

Nature's Choice - Barbara's Bakery, Petaluma, CA (707) 765-2273

Wheat-free, gluten free flour, no sugar, additives - David's Good Batter, P.O. Box 102, Bausman, PA, 17504 (717) 872-0652

Living Lightly - Non-Dairy Dessert, Turtle Mountain, (503) 998-6778

Tofu & Soya Waffles - Toffles, DAE Han Inc. (503) 233-TOFU

SOLAIT Powdered Soya Bean, P.O.Box 885, Carroll, IA 51401 (800) 747-8605

Mori-Nu Tofu & Soya Bean Curd, Morinaga Nut Foods, Inc., 2050 W. 190th Street, Suite #110, Torrance, CA 90504

Soya Milk (and other products) Shiloh Farms, 438 White Oak Road, New Holland, PA 17557 (800) 829-5100 (they will send a catalogue)

Vita Soy - soya drinks - 22 Park Lane, Brisbane CA 94005 (800) VitaSoY

Natural & Organic Foods ~ Soya products - Heartland Foods, R.Rt. 2, Box 189B, Susquehanna, PA 18847 (717) 879~8790 Lucy Wilson Sherman

Dairy free canola oil spread - Spectrum Spread, Spectrum Naturals (707) 778-8900

Dairy free Ice Cream Substitute - Imagine Foods "Rice Dream"

Tofutti's "Better Than Cream Cheese" (soya), (909) 272~2400

West Soy, Light non-dairy Creamer, (301) 886-8200

Gensing Extractum - Root to Health, Hsu's Ginseng Enterprises, Inc. and Farms, P.O. Box 509, Wausau, WI 54402-0509

INTRODUCTION

This book has been specially written for those who, for one reason or another, cannot tolerate eggs, milk, cheese, butter, wheat flour, chocolate, salt, sugar beet, sugar cane, baking powder or cornflour.

As someone who cannot tolerate dairy produce, I know how difficult it is to prepare meals for a family and then try to find a suitable well-balanced meal for the odd one out.

It seemed to me that the answer to such a problem was to find recipes to suit all the family but use a replacement such as soya milk (as in my own case). So it was purely self-preservation that led me, over the years, to create these recipes that can be eaten by everyone, as well as the person who has to find alternative ingredients to replace the normal basics.

All the meals are economical and not expensive to prepare, while most of the recipes are quick and easy - the vegetables being simply prepared and needing very little cooking, thus preserving all their goodness.

I am not attempting to offer any diagnoses, as I assume you already know the type of food most likely to cause trouble. However, there is a very simple and fairly reliable way of finding out the cause of a complaint, which is to leave out one of the foods mentioned above each week. If the trouble recurs, then it could be that food. Try it again: if the complaint disappears again, drop the item from your diet and mention it to your doctor.

All the recipes in this book are written in such a way that they can be adapted to any of the replacements mentioned above, the choice is yours. However, if you are allergic or cannot tolerate just one item find the replacement for that first, then use conventional ingredients and follow the recipe.

HINTS

ALFALFA You will see alfalfa noted many times in various recipes. This is because it is almost a complete food for goodness, as well as being easy to grow. Although alfalfa is best eaten raw, it can be put into soups and stews. I like it best in a salad or sandwich.

GARLIC A lot of savory recipes include garlic. This is a good disinfectant for the stomach, but leaves a pungent smell on the breath, which is why many people shun it. To be rid of the smell, eat a sprig of parsley at the end of the meal. As parsley is full of iron, this is doubly good for you!

WATER Drink lots of clean water. Not only will you have bright eyes, but it helps flush out the kidneys, bowels and bladder. If you find that your local tap water tastes flat or smells too heavily of chlorine, drink spa water, preferably bottled in glass.

EXERCISE Get plenty of exercise if possible. This will tone up the system and stimulate the circulation.

FRUIT Eat plenty of fruit and vegetables, also salads. These are not fattening and contain many vitamins and minerals required by the body.

DIET Do try to vary your diet as much as possible, using different recipes each day. For instance, substitute Fructose for pure maple syrup if you can tolerate it. Better still, do without sweeteners for one day. New foods are appearing on the market all the time, so look around Asian, Chinese and Health Food stores.

COELIACS Although this book was not written with coeliacs in mind especially, most of the recipes are suitable for their diet. It is wise for this group of people to look through the book and pick out the most suitable recipes for them, always being on the lookout for new products that can be used in place of those mentioned.

OVEN TEMPERATURES

°F	°C	Gas Mark	Temperature
250	130	½	Very cool
275	140	1	Very cool
300	150	2	Cool
325	165	3	Warm
350	180	4	Moderate
375	190	5	Fairly hot
400	200	6	Fairly hot
425	215	7	Hot
450	230	8	Very hot
475	240	9	Very hot

All the recipes in this book are worked out in
British
American
and Continental measures

Oven temperatures are in electric and gas

Unless otherwise mentioned
all the recipes are for two servings

ABBREVIATIONS

pt = pint
tblsp = tablespoon
teasp = teaspoon
oz = ounce
lb = pound
mins = minutes
g = grams
ml = millilitres

SOYA CONVERSION TABLE

COOKED PUDDINGS Dilute equal parts of soya milk with water. Use in ordinary way and add to recipe.

SAUCES Dilute equal parts of soya milk with water and use in cooked sauces. Ensure that it is stirred well before mixing with other ingredients.

SOUPS Dilute equal parts of soya milk with water. Stir well and add to soup near the end of cooking. Do not re boil soup after adding soya milk.

SMALL CAKES AND BUNS Use one tablespoonful of soya milk to two tablespoonfuls of water. Mix well and use in ordinary way, following recipe.

LARGE CAKES Dilute equal parts of soya milk with water. Mix well, use in ordinary way, following recipe.

TEA, COFFEE AND CAROB Soya milk can be used undiluted with some success, but only if the beverage is not too strong or too hot. The acid in these drinks causes the natural protein to give the appearance that it has curdled or gone sour. This is not so, but it gives an unpleasant appearance to the drink. On the other hand, soya cream is very pleasant in all three beverages, but can only be added when the drink is cool enough to consume; added before, it will curdle.

WHIPPED CREAM   2 tblsp soya cream

1 teasp Potato flour or rice flour

Icing sugar to taste [see page 94]

Have ready a large pan of boiling water. Into either an enamel saucepan or a fireproof dish, mix flour and cream with a wooden spoon (if metal comes into contact with this cream it will blacken). Stir until smooth and creamy. Put dish or saucepan into boiling water stirring constantly to prevent lumps forming. It takes about 3 minutes to thicken. Remove from heat and continue to stir until cool. Add icing sugar and stir until smooth. When the mixture has cooled it can be piped on to puddings, pies or cakes in the normal way. [If you have a double boiler in enamel, this will save a lot of bother in cooking

FRUIT SALADS AND COLD DESSERTS Delicious with soya cream straight from the tin. It is not quite as thick as whipped cream, but I find it very palatable without any extra sweetening, although a little powdered Fructose may be added. 1 can of soya cream is 16 oz or 169 ml.

Plamil soya milk is a little more concentrated than other soya milk, which makes it more economical

INSTRUCTIONS FOR SELECTING YOUR CHOICE
OF FOOD REPLACEMENTS

1. All these recipes are created without eggs, which should therefore not be added under any circumstances.
2. Very few people are allergic or intolerant to all the common ingredients. The idea is to use normal foodstuffs, then select the replacement you require.
3. Assuming that you cannot tolerate (for example) flour: use all the normal ingredients, but replace ordinary flour with Trufree or Nutricia (Rite-Diet) and proceed, following the recipe with everyday ingredients. The latter requires a little extra water added to recipes where flour is needed.
Sample recipe

PINEAPPLE CANDY CAKE
Replacements can be used for
4 oz   Flour (can use Trufree or similar brand)
2 oz   Fat (can use Vitaquell or similar brand)
2 oz   Sugar (can use Fructose)
2 tblsp   Cold tea (can use Rooibosch)
Pinch Salt (can use Ruthmol or similar brand)
Conventional ingredients
1 oz   Crystallised fruit (see recipe)
1 teasp   Pectin
Few drops Almond essence
1 tblsp   Water
The full recipe can be found on page 109.

These recipes are very economical, full of nutrition, as well as being attractive. They are also suitable for vegetarians.

GLOSSARY OF REPLACEMENT INGREDIENTS

MILK & CREAM Soya milk and cream from **Plamil** Foods, Ltd. (Plamil House, Bowles Well Gardens, Folkestone, Kent CT19 6PQ [0303 850588]), who have a mail order service; **Granose** Products (Haldane foods Group, Howard Way, Newport Pagnell, Buckinghamshire MK16 9PY [0905 211311]); a few of the larger Superstores; Holland & Barrett branches; and most Health Food stores.

BUTTER/MARGARINE Vitaquell (polyunsaturated, salt free, contains wheat germ and corn oil) (Fauser Vitaquell, 2 Hamburg 54, Germany) from Holland & Barrett; also soya margarine from **Roys** of Wroxham; Holland & Barrett; J Sainsbury; Health Food stores and **Granose** Products. Read list of ingredients on cartons, as some contain salt.

CHEESE Soya Cottage Cheese Spread (see also recipe on page 74 of this book). Also soya cheese spread from **Plamil** Foods, Ltd. (not suitable for all diets).

FLOUR Trufree self raising and plain flour (gluten, grain, albumen and additive free) from **Trufree** Foods (Larkhalls Natural Health, Putney Bridge Road, London SW15 2PY [081-874 1130]), who have a mail order service in Great Britain, also obtained from Holland & Barrett or on prescription from your GP (where necessary). **Nutricia** Dietary Products (494-496 Honeypot Lane, Stanmore, Middlesex HA7 1JH [081-951 5155]) also make flour suitable for gluten free diets and also suitable for some other cases; they also have a mail order service in Great Britain and the United States of America.

SAUCE THICKENERS Potato and rice flour from **Trufree** Foods, also Nutricia Dietary Products. Both have a mail order service.

BAKING POWDER Salfree from **Trufree** Foods, Ltd., and **Nutricia** Dietary Products. Both have a mail order service.

7

SUGAR Fructose fruit sugar from **Trufree** Foods, Ltd., who have a mail order service.
SALT Ruthmol (sodium free, contains wheat starch) from **Trufree** Foods.
CHOCOLATE Carob powder (grain & gluten free) from **Trufree** Foods, Ltd.
PECTIN Pectin (grain & gluten free) from **Trufree** Foods, Ltd.
TEA Rooibosch tea bags (caffeine free and low tannin content) from most Health Food stores.
COFFEE Hag or dandelion coffee (caffeine free) from most Health Food stores, Holland & Barrett branches and some Supermarkets.
GELATINE Gelazone or Agar Agar (starch free) from most Health Food stores and Holland & Barrett branches.

Trufree Foods supply an information handbook on request. Nutricia, Granose and Plamil also issue information leaflets on products available, obtainable on request. Most of the larger supermarkets issue lists of foods that they sell which are suitable for people on restricted diets and can be obtained on request.

Further information about allergies can be obtained from
  Mrs Nathan Hill
  Action Against Allergy
  43 The Downs
  London S W 20
  (Telephone: 081-947 5082)

SOUPS AND STARTERS

CELERY SOUP

1 pt	Vegetable juice	(2½ cups - 600ml)
4/6	Outer stalks of celery (washed & chopped)	
1	Small onion (peeled & chopped)	
1 clove	Garlic (skinned & chopped)	
	Salt & pepper to taste	

Put all ingredients into saucepan. Bring to boil, then simmer for 20 mins. Put soup through blender or sieve. Reheat; serve with croutons or crackers [recipe pages 86 or 90].

CREAM OF MUSHROOM SOUP

8 oz	Mushrooms (chopped: save some for garnishing)	(2 cups - 225g)
1½ pt	Water	
1	Small onion (peeled & chopped)	
1 teasp	Salt	
4 tblsp	Margarine	
4 tblsp	Flour	
½pt	Soya milk	(1¼ cups - 300ml)
¼ teasp	Pepper	
Pinch	Paprika	

Put ingredients, except flour, some mushrooms and milk, in pan. Cover with water, boil for 2 mins. Turn down and simmer for 20 mins. Add flour mixed with a little water. Boil for another 5 mins. Put through blender or sieve. Lightly brown slices of mushroom reserved for garnish. Add to soup. Bring back to boil for 5 mins. Finally, add milk and boil gently for 3 mins, stirring to prevent burning.

CREAM OF VEGETABLE SOUP

1 can   Soya cream
½pt   Home made vegetable soup   (1¼ cups - 300ml)
1 tblsp Sunflower oil
Pinch   Cayenne pepper or paprika and salt

Put soup through blender or sieve when cool. Return to saucepan, bring to boil. Add extra flavouring, like a good pinch of pepper or salt. Gradually add the cream by folding it in gently. Bring to boil for 1 min, stirring gently to prevent sticking. Serve with croutons [see recipe page 90].

LETTUCE SOUP

1 pt   Vegetable juice (2½ cups - 600ml)
6/8   Large lettuce leaves (washed)
1 clove   Garlic (skinned & chopped)
1   Small onion (peeled & sliced)
2 teasp [heaped]   Potato flour
1 tblsp   Sunflower oil
                      Salt & pepper to taste

Put all ingredients into saucepan. Bring to boil, turn down and simmer for 20 mins. Cool and put through blender or sieve. Reheat and serve with croutons [see page 90].

PARSLEY SOUP

1 oz   Flour   (1 tblsp- 25g)
1 oz   Margarine
4 oz   Potato (peeled & chopped)   (4 tblsp - 100g)
2 teasp   Parsley (chopped, inc. stalks)   (10g)
1½ pt   Water   (3¾ cups - 900ml)
½ pt   Soya milk   (1¼ cups - 300ml)
1   Small onion (skinned & sliced)

Salt & pepper to taste

Put all ingredients, except flour, milk and soya margarine, in saucepan. Boil for 20 mins. Remove from heat and put through blender or sieve. Melt margarine, blend in flour. Gradually add the soup and boil for a further 3 mins. Lastly, add milk, boil 3 mins, stirring constantly to prevent burning.

VEGETABLE SOUP

2 pt	Water	(5 cups - 120ml)
1	Bouquet garni	
2	Carrots (scraped & chopped)	
1	Large onion (peeled & sliced)	
1 stick	Celery	
2 teasp **each**	Split peas, Pearl barley, Lentils	
2 tblsp **each**	Ming, Butter, and Marrow fat beans	
Pinch **each**	Oregano, Basil, Cardamon seeds, Onion seeds	
	Salt & pepper to taste	

Put all ingredients into saucepan and bring to boil. Turn down heat and simmer for 2 hours. Remove bouquet garni and serve.

BUTTER BEAN PATÉ

4 oz	Butter beans (soaked overnight)	(¼ cup - 125g)
1	Medium onion (peeled & chopped)	
1 tblsp	Sunflower or soya oil	
1	Medium tomato (blanched & de-seeded)	
1 teasp	Paprika	
1 teasp	Curry powder	
1 tblsp [level]	Chopped parsley	
1 clove	Garlic (skinned & chopped) [optional]	
1 tblsp	Lemon juice	
1 tblsp	Water	

Cover beans with fresh water in saucepan, bring to boil, reduce heat and simmer for ½ hour. Drain off water and cool. Mince or purée beans in a food processor. Lightly brown onion and tomato in oil in shallow pan, then mince or purée. Mix all ingredients, then scoop mixture into a previously oiled 7" oven-proof dish, cover with foil and bake for 1 hour.

Electric 180°C 370°F Gas mark 4 Just above centre

MAIN COURSES

APPLE AND ONION FLAN WITH HERB SAUCE

	Pastry No. 1 [see page 76]
1 tblsp	Haricot beans (soaked overnight)
1	Onion (peeled & minced)
1	Cooking apple (peeled, cored and minced)
1 tblsp	Sultanas (soaked for 1 hour previously)
1 tblsp	Lemon juice
¼	Red pepper (washed, deseeded & minced)
1 teasp	Mustard seeds
1 clove	Garlic (skinned & chopped)
2 teasp	Potato flour
5 oz	Mixed vegetable juice (⅔ cup - 150ml)
Pinch	Marjoram, sage, cayenne pepper
Little	Alfalfa or watercress for garnishing
	Salt to taste

Put beans in fresh water, bring to boil, reduce heat and simmer for ½ hour. Drain, put in bowl with apple, onion, sultanas, garlic, pepper, juice and salt. Roll out pastry and line a 7 inch flan tin. Spoon mixture into flan case. Any left-over pastry cut into strips and crisscross over top of flan. Put flan on baking sheet and bake for ½ hour.

200° electric 400°F Gas Mark 6 Just above centre

SAUCE:
Mix vegetable juice with herbs and mustard seeds in a saucepan, bring to boil, reduce heat and simmer for a couple of minutes. Mix potato flour and a little cold water into a thick paste and stir into juice until it thickens and is smooth. Pour over flan. Garnish

13

AUBERGINE WITH CABBAGE FRITTERS

2 tblsp	Pinto beans (soaked overnight)
1 tblsp	Hazelnuts (minced)
1	Large aubergine (peeled & sliced lengthwise)
2	Mushrooms (chopped)
1	Medium onion (peeled & minced)
½	Red pepper (washed, deseeded & minced)
½	Small white cabbage (finely shredded)
6 tblsp	Sunflower oil
¼ teasp	Mustard seeds
Pinch	Coriander, paprika, turmeric
	Salt to taste

Drain beans, cover with fresh water in pan, bring to boil, reduce heat and simmer for ½ hour. Add salt. Heat little oil in pan and add nuts, mushroom, onion and pepper. Cook until onion softens and becomes transparent, add herbs and mustard seeds; stir well. Drain and mince beans and add to other ingredients, except cabbage and aubergine. Put each aubergine half in foil that is slightly higher than aubergine. Spoon bean mixture into each half. Put in oiled casserole and bake ¾ hour.

200° electric 400°F Gas Mark 6 Just above centre

CABBAGE FRITTERS:
Put cabbage shreds in boiling oil for a couple of seconds, until crispy, but not too brown.

ASPARAGUS FLAN WITH PEACH SAUCE

	Pastry No. 1 [see page 76]
2 tblsp	Blackeye beans (soaked overnight)
8 oz	Asparagus (woody ends trimmed) (225g)
2	Medium peaches (blanched, halved & stoned)
1 tblsp	Fructose
Pinch	Fenugreek seeds (crushed), paprika, nutmeg, chives

14

1 teasp	Potato flour
1 teasp	Margarine
	Salt & pepper to taste

Put beans in pan covered with fresh water, bring to boil, reduce heat and simmer for ½ hour. Remove beans and use water to boil asparagus that has been tied in small bundles for 10 mins. Drain and put on tissue until wanted. Make up pastry and line a well oiled 7 inch flan tin. Crimp edges of pastry. Mince beans, add fenugreek and pepper. Spread beans over pastry, then lay asparagus in a wheel design, with heads to the centre, slightly raised, like a flower. Dot with margarine and sprinkle with paprika. Season with salt. Bake for ½ hour.

200° electric 400°F Gas Mark 6 Near top

PEACH SAUCE:
Blanch peaches in boiling water, remove skins, slice and discard stones. Add pinch of nutmeg and chives to slices. Mix flour with a little water to make a thick paste, stir with peaches and boil gently until clear - about 5 mins. Pour over flan.

AUNT ETHEL'S SPECIALITY

4 oz	Mushrooms	(1 cup - 125g)
½	Small red pepper (deseeded & sliced)	
2 tblsp	Soya oil	
¼ pt	Water	(⅔ cup - 150ml)
1 teasp	Fructose	
1 tblsp	Mustard seeds	
1 tblsp	Mild curry powder	
1	Large onion (peeled & sliced)	
2	Medium tomatoes (blanched & deseeded)	
1	Banana (sliced lengthwise)	
	Margarine	
Pinch	Ginger	
	Salt & pepper to taste	

Brown onion in margarine until transparent, add pepper. Chop tomatoes and add to onion and pepper with other ingredients, except banana. Bring to boil in large pan, reduce heat and simmer for 5 mins. Thicken with a little rice flour. Fry banana slices in a little soya oil until brown, then add to sauce. Serve with rice or jacket potato.

AUNT ETHEL'S SPICED SUPPER LOAF

16 oz	Mixed vegetables, such as
	2 mushrooms (washed & chopped)
	1 carrot (scraped & chopped)
	1 stick of celery (washed & chopped)
	½ small swede or turnip (peeled & chopped)
	1 small red pepper (deseeded & chopped)
1 tblsp	Sunflower or soya oil
100g	Packet of unsalted peanuts and raisins
1 tblsp	Rice flour
1 tblsp	Water
4 oz	Breadcrumbs (home made) (1 cup - 100g)
	Medium onion (peeled & chopped)
½ teasp	Rosemary }
¼ teasp	Marjoram } or 1½ teasp mixed herbs
Pinch	Thyme }
	Salt & pepper to taste

Put all chopped vegetables into food processor with nuts and raisins and grind finely. Lightly fry onion in oil. Stir all ingredients together. Oil a 2lb bread tin and scoop in mixture. Bake for 1 hour.

100° electric   370°F Gas Mark 4 Just above centre

AVOCADO PEAR RISOTTO

4 oz	Butter beans (soaked overnight) (1 cup - 100g)	
4 oz	Mushrooms (chopped)	
4 oz	Rice	
2 oz	Peas	(½ cup - 50g)
2 oz	Carrots	
1	Onion (peeled & chopped)	
½	Red pepper (washed, deseeded & chopped)	
1 tblsp	Sunflower oil	
1	Avocado pear	
Pinch	Turmeric	
Little	Margarine	
	Salt to taste	

Put beans in fresh water, bring to boil, reduce heat and simmer for ¾ hour, season with salt. Drain and mince finely. Meanwhile, cook peas and carrots for 10 mins. Heat oil and lightly brown pepper, onion and mushroom, add to other vegetables, mix well. Boil rice with turmeric until soft, drain and put in fireproof dish, spoon vegetables into centre. Keep warm in oven. Peel avocado pear, discard stone, coat with margarine and arrange on top of bean mixture.

BUTTER BEAN AND APRICOT SAVORY ROLLS WITH SPICE SAUCE

2 oz	Butter beans (soaked overnight) (½ cup - 50g)	
4	Dried apricots (soaked overnight)	
1 tblsp	Mixed nuts (chopped)	
½ teasp	Horseradish (ground)	
¼ teasp	Mustard seeds	
Pinch	Paprika, marjoram, cayenne, thyme, mace	
6 oz	Pastry No. 1 [see page 76]	(175g)
	Salt to taste	

Put beans and apricots in saucepan, cover with water, bring to boil, reduce heat and simmer for 15 mins. Drain and mince finely, season with salt. Mix all other ingredients, but pastry. Roll pastry out on floured board and cut into 4 equal parts. Spread bean mixture equally in centre of each piece. Roll up and dampen edges, then seal with water. Prick the top of each roll. Put on oiled baking sheet and bake for ¾ hour.

200° electric 400°F Gas Mark 6 Near top

SPICE SAUCE:

½ pt	Mixed vegetable juice (1¼ cups - 300ml)
4 oz	Mushrooms (minced) (1 cup - 100g)
1	Small red pepper (washed, deseeded & chopped)
1 tblsp	Potato flour
2 tblsp	Sunflower oil
1 teasp	Mustard seeds
1	Large onion (peeled & minced)
Pinch	Ginger, oregano
	Salt to taste

Mix flour with a little juice, add rest of ingredients in a saucepan, bring to boil, reduce heat and simmer for 15 mins. Serve with savory rolls.

COUNTRY STIR FRY

½ pt	Water (1¼ cups - 300ml)
1	Onion (peeled & chopped)
4 oz	Mixed vegetables (chopped) (¾ cup - 125g)
1	Courgette (washed & sliced)
2 tblsp	Sunflower or soya oil
2 tblsp	Mixed chopped nuts
4 oz	Mushrooms (1¼ cups - 125g)
1 teasp [heaped]	Potato flour
1	Large potato (sliced)
Pinch	Fennel, mace
Little	Parsley, chives (chopped)

18

Salt & pepper to taste

Lightly brown onion with oil in shallow pan. Brown potato slices in oil and leave in warm oven. Add all other ingredients to onion, bring to boil, reduce heat and simmer for 5 mins. Place potato on top and serve with rice.

COUNTRY PIE

2 oz	Butter beans (soaked overnight)	(¼ cup - 50g)
4 oz	Mushrooms (sliced)	(1 cup - 125g)
½ pt	Water	(1¼ cups - 300ml)
1	Medium onion (peeled & chopped)	
1 tblsp	Cashew nuts	
2 tblsp	Red or green peppers (deseeded & chopped)	
1 clove	Garlic (skinned & chopped)	
1	Large tomato (blanched & chopped)	
½ teasp	Mustard seeds (crushed)	
1 tblsp	Sunflower or soya oil	
6 oz	Potato (mashed)	(½ cup - 175g)
	Salt & pepper to taste	

Lightly brown onion in oil, put into oven-proof dish and add all other ingredients. Cover top with mashed potato. Dot all over with a little margarine. Bake for 1 hour.
200° electric   400°F Gas Mark 6 Just above centre

COURGETTES STUFFED WITH SAVORY PRUNES SERVED WITH BEAN SPROUTS AND PEAS

2	Courgettes (washed)	
8	Prunes (washed, stoned & soaked overnight)	
10 oz	Potato (cooked & mashed)	(1 cup - 275g)
¼	Green pepper (washed, deseeded & minced)	
1	Small onion (peeled & chopped)	
1 handful	Bean sprouts (washed)	

1 tblsp	Sunflower oil
Little	Margarine
Pinch	Cayenne pepper, paprika
	Salt to taste

Peel courgettes and slice in half lengthwise. Mince half of onion (reserving rest for bean sprouts). Mix onion, pepper, prune pulp, salt and cayenne; spoon into courgette halves. Put in small casserole to hold them firm. Put knob of margarine on each, cover. Bake for 1 hour. Lastly, add salt.

200° electric   400°F Gas Mark 6   Near top

Remove from oven, pipe mashed potato over each piece, sprinkle with paprika and brown under grill. Meanwhile, lightly brown rest of onion in hot oil, add bean sprouts and stir for about 5 mins. Serve with courgettes.

CURRIED VEGETABLES AND RICE

1	Onion (peeled & chopped)
1	Medium potato (peeled & chopped)
2 tblsp	Peas
2 tblsp	Green beans (finely sliced)
2 tblsp	Mushrooms (chopped)
1 tblsp	Sultanas (washed)
1 clove	Garlic (skinned & crushed)
2	Large tomatoes (blanched, skinned & depipped)
2 tblsp	Garam-masala [see below]
Pinch	Ginger, chili powder
1 tblsp	Sunflower oil
	Juice of 1 lemon
	Salt to taste
4 tblsp	Rice

Lightly brown onion in oil. Add other ingredients, except salt and rice. Bring to boil, reduce heat and simmer for 20 mins. Add salt.

20

GARAM-MASALA:

2 tblsp **each** of Peppercorns, coriander, caraway seeds
2 teasp **each** of Cloves, cinnamon
20   Cardamoms
Remove skins from cardamoms and put all ingredients in a coffee grinder or grind with mortar and pestle.

Cover rice with water, bring to boil, reduce heat and simmer until soft, about 10 mins. Season with salt. Drain and serve with curry immediately.

CABBAGE PARCELS
WITH PRUNE PURÉE AND MASHED POTATO

16	Outer leaves of white cabbage (washed)
8 oz	Potato (cooked & mashed) (1 cup - 225g)
12	Dried prunes (washed & destoned)
1	Small onion (peeled & chopped)
1 level dessertspoonful Fructose	
1 tblsp	Margarine
Pinch	Rosemary, basil, mace
Few sprigs	Parsley
	Salt to taste

Put prunes in saucepan, cover with water, bring to boil, reduce heat, cover and simmer for 20 mins. Add Fructose and simmer for further 5 mins. Pour off juice and reserve in bowl. Put pruned in liquidiser or through a sieve and return to juice. Simmer onions in hot oil until transparent. To make parcels, put 4 leaves on top of each other. Add herbs to onion and divide equally between the parcels. Roll each up and put in oiled casserole. Pour prune purée over parcels. Dot with margarine. Cover and bake for ½ hour. Season with salt.
        200° electric 400°F Gas Mark 6 Near top
 Serve with potato rosettes.
To make rosettes, put finely mashed potato in an icing bag and

21

pipe large rosettes on to a well oiled baking sheet, making about 8. Put them under grill to brown. Garnish with parsley. Serve immediately with cabbage parcels.

RED CABBAGE WITH SPICED APPLE AND MINI BUTTER BEAN ROLLS

1	Small red cabbage (washed & sliced)
1 tblsp	Butter beans (soaked overnight)
1 tblsp	Fructose
1 tblsp	Sunflower seeds
1 teasp	Potato flour
1	Medium apple (peeled, cored & chopped)
1	Small onion (peeled & chopped)
1 tblsp	Soya milk
Pinch	Basil, rosemary, cumin seeds, nutmeg
	Juice of 1 orange
	Pastry No. 1 [see page 76]
	Salt to taste

Cover beans with water in pan, bring to boil, reduce heat and simmer for 1 hour. Put cabbage in pan, pour in enough water to come up to middle of pan. Bring to boil, reduce heat and simmer for 10 mins. Strain cabbage through colander and put in well oiled casserole. Squeeze orange juice over cabbage. Put apple in saucepan with a little water to cover bottom of pan, simmer for 5 mins, flavour with nutmeg and Fructose. Mix flour with a little water to a thick paste. Pour over cabbage, bake for ½ hour. Season with salt.
200° electric   400°F Gas Mark 6 Just above centre
Mince beans finely and put in bowl. Heat oil and lightly brown onion, add to beans, sprinkle in herbs, crush sunflower seeds in coffee grinder or mincer and mix with beans. Roll pastry out and cut into 4 inch squares. Spoon mixture equally over and seal with a little water. Brush with a little soya milk. Put rolls on well oiled baking sheet and bake until brown.
        220° electric 425°F Gas Mark 7 Near top

22

CELERY STUFFED WITH NUTS AND PINEAPPLE

1 heaped tblsp	Pinto beans (soaked overnight)
1 heaped tblsp	Mushrooms (chopped)
1 heaped tblsp	Pineapple (minced)
1 tblsp	Vegetable juice
1 bunch	Celery (washed & sectioned)
1 clove	Garlic (skinned & crushed)
½	Red pepper (deseeded & minced)
1 tblsp	Mixed nuts
Pinch	Basil, oregano, cayenne pepper, marjoram
	Salt to taste

Cover beans in saucepan with fresh water, bring to boil, reduce heat and simmer for ½ hour. Drain and put into bowl, adding rest of ingredients, except celery; mix well. Cut celery into 4 inch pieces, then spoon bean mixture into them, pressing well down into each piece. Arrange in well oiled casserole, season with salt, cover and bake for 1½ hours.

200° electric 400°F Gas Mark 6 Centre

COTTAGE PIE

1 tblsp	Pinto or blackeye beans (soaked overnight)	
2	Large mushrooms (chopped)	
	Large tomato (blanched, skinned, depipped & chopped)	
8 oz	Potato (cooked & mashed)	(1 cup - 225g)
1 tblsp	Sunflower oil	
1 tblsp	Margarine	
Pinch	Rosemary, oregano, paprika	
Few sprigs	Parsley	
	Salt & pepper to taste	

Put beans in saucepan with fresh water, bring to boil, reduce heat and simmer for ½ hour. Drain and mince, put in bowl with

23

herbs. Heat oil in pan and lightly brown onion. Add onion, tomato and mushroom to beans and mix well. Oil casserole and spoon bean mixture over bottom, spread mashed potato on top, dot with margarine, season with salt, and bake for ½ hour.

190° electric 375°F Gas Mark 5   Near top

If not quite brown, finish under grill. Garnish with parsley.

EASTERN MEDLEY

3	Medium mushrooms (chopped)
1 tblsp	Sunflower or soya oil
1 tblsp	Red pepper (deseeded & chopped)
2	Medium tomatoes (chopped)
2 sticks	Celery (chopped finely)
1 tblsp	Sultanas
1 tblsp	Currants
1	Onion (peeled & chopped)
1 clove	Garlic (skinned & crushed)
1 teasp	Curry powder
½ teasp	Mustard seeds (crushed)
1 teasp	Potato flour
½ pt	Water (1¼ cups - 300ml)
Pinch	Marjoram, basil, oregano
	Salt & pepper to taste

Lightly brown onion in oil. Add all other ingredients, except potato flour. Bring to boil, reduce heat and simmer for 7 mins. Sprinkle potato flour over top and stir well for 1 further min. Serve with rice.

STUFFED MARROW
SERVED WITH MEDITERRANEAN SAUCE

1 heaped tblsp	Blackeye beans (soaked overnight)
1 heaped tblsp	Mushrooms (minced)
1	Medium marrow (peeled & centre pulp removed)
1	Small onion (peeled & sliced)
½	Red pepper (washed, deseeded & minced)
1 clove	Garlic (skinned & crushed)
½ teasp	Sesame seeds (crushed)
Pinch	Mixed herbs, chives
	Salt to taste
	Mediterranean sauce [see page 76]

Cover beans in pan with fresh water, bring to boil, reduce heat and simmer for ½ hour. Drain and pour into bowl. Add rest of ingredients, except marrow, salt and sesame seeds. Cut marrow into quarters and spoon bean mixture equally into each section. Sprinkle with sesame seeds. Put sections into well oiled casserole with just enough water to cover bottom of dish. Season with salt and bake for 1 hour.

200° electric   400°F Gas Mark 6 Just above centre
Serve with Mediterranean sauce [see page 76].

MIXED VEGETABLE PUDDING

8 oz	Mixed dried beans & peas (soaked overnight) (1 cup - 225g)
1	Large onion (peeled & chopped)
1	Carrot (scraped & chopped)
3 sticks	Celery (washed & chopped)
4 tblsp	Mixed vegetable juice
1 clove	Garlic (skinned & chopped)
Pinch	Oregano, basil, rosemary
	Pastry No. 2 [see page 77]
	Salt & pepper to taste

Roll pastry on lightly floured board to about 1 inch thick. Drain water from beans & peas and put all ingredients in well oiled pudding basin, topping with pastry. Cover with foil, leaving a pleat in the middle to let pudding rise, tie with string. Put in pan of boiling water halfway up basin, cover with lid and steam for 2 hours. Check occasionally to see pan has not boiled dry.

PEPPERS STUFFED WITH WESTERN BARBECUE SAUCE

2	Large red peppers (caps removed & deseeded)
1	Small onion (peeled & minced)
1 tblsp	Sesame seeds (ground or minced)
1 clove	Garlic (skinned & crushed)
	Western barbecue sauce [see page 75]
	Salt & pepper to taste

Put peppers into well oiled casserole and cover with rest of ingredients. Add a little water. Cover and bake for 35-40 mins.
          180° electric   350°F Gas Mark 5 Just above centre
Serve with Western barbecue sauce [see page 75].

MIXED VEGETABLE STEW WITH CROUTONS AND RICE

1	Leek (washed & sliced)	
4	Large mushrooms (chopped)	
1	Onion (peeled & chopped)	
1	Large carrot (scraped & chopped)	
1	Small swede (peeled & chopped)	
3 sticks	Celery (washed & chopped)	
1 clove	Garlic (skinned & chopped)	
1 tblsp	Sesame seeds	
1 bunch	Watercress	
3 oz	Rice	(½ cup - 75g)
	Croutons [see page 90]	

Salt, pepper, oregano, rosemary, marjoram, basil to taste

26

Cover all ingredients, except rice and salt, with water in a shallow pan with lid and simmer for ½ hour on low heat. Cover rice with water, season with salt and boil for 12 mins. Drain and put in warm dish, pour vegetables in centre. Sprinkle with croutons.

PAT'S VEGETABLE COBBLER

2 oz	Pinto beans (soaked overnight)
1	Medium parsnip (peeled & chopped)
1 tblsp	Sunflower or soya oil
1 tblsp	Potato flour
¼ tblsp	Mustard seeds (crushed)
½ teasp	Sage
½ teasp	Mixed herbs
1 clove	Garlic (skinned & crushed)
1	Medium carrot (scraped & chopped)
1	Medium onion (skinned & chopped)
½ pt	Water (1¼ cups - 300ml)
	Salt & pepper to taste
	Pastry No.2 [see page 77]

Drain beans and scoop into oven-proof dish, add all other ingredients, except pastry. Roll out pastry. Using a 2" pastry cutter, make pastry rounds and arrange these on top of dish. Bake for 1 hour.

220° electric   425°F Gas Mark 7   Centre oven

PINEKERNEL STUFFED ROAST

1 tblsp	Pine kernels (ground)
1	Small onion (peeled & chopped)
1 tblsp	Hazelnuts or Cashew nuts (finely chopped)
1 tblsp	Sesame seeds (ground)
1 tblsp	Mixed vegetable juice
1 teasp	Potato flour
1 tblsp	Sunflower oil

Pinch	Chopped chives, basil, rosemary
	Salt to taste
	Alfalfa or watercress for garnishing

Heat oil in pan and simmer onion until it becomes transparent. Add other ingredients, except flour and vegetable juice. Mix latter to smooth paste and blend into other ingredients. Spoon roast mixture into well oiled casserole.

STUFFING:

2 tblsp	Chestnuts (boiled, peeled & minced)
1 stick	Celery (minced)
1 tblsp	Mushrooms (minced)
1 tblsp	Breadcrumbs (home-made)
Pinch	Oregano, basil, sage, parsley
	Salt & pepper to taste

Boil chestnuts 20 mins, drain, peel, mince, mix with other ingredients. Put in centre of roast and bake for 40 mins.
200° electric 425°F Gas mark 7 Just above centre
Garnish with parsley, serve sauce of your own choice.

This recipe makes a fine Christmas dinner.

POTATO AND FENNEL CROQUETTES
WITH EASTERN RICE

2 tblsp	Lentils (soaked overnight)	
3 oz	Rice	(1 cup - 75g)
10 oz	Potato (Mashed)	(1 cup - 275g)
1 tblsp	Fresh fennel (washed & minced)	
1 tblsp	Cucumber (peeled & minced)	
1 clove	Garlic (skinned & crushed)	
1	Small onion (peeled & minced)	
¼	Red pepper (washed, deseeded & minced)	
1 tblsp	Hazelnuts (shelled & minced)	
¼ teasp	Curry powder	

2 tblsp	Plain flour
2 tblsp	Soya milk
Pinch	Mixed herbs, rosemary, cayenne, turmeric
	Salt to taste
	Watercress for garnishing

Cover lentils in pan with fresh water and boil gently for ½ hour, drain and mince. Mix ingredients, except rice, cayenne, turmeric, flour salt and watercress, together. Roll mixture into sausage shapes, brush with soya milk, roll in flour. Put croquettes in well oiled casserole and bake for ¾ hour.

200° electric 400°F Gas Mark 6   Near top
If not quite brown, finish under grill.

EASTERN RICE:
Cover rice with water in saucepan, add cayenne and turmeric. Boil gently for 12 mins or until soft. Drain, put on large warm plate, season with salt, arrange croquettes round dish and garnish with watercress.

POTATO AND MIXED VEGETABLE MINI-ROLLS
SERVED WITH MIXED VEGETABLES

3 oz	Potato (cooked & mashed)	(¾ cup - 75g)
2	Mushrooms (chopped)	
1	Tomato (chopped)	
1 stick	Celery (washed & chopped)	
1	Small carrot (scraped & chopped finely)	
1	Onion (peeled & chopped)	
8 oz Packet	Frozen Mixed vegetables (prepared & chopped)	
	(1 cup - 225g)	
1 tblsp	Sunflower oil	
1 tblsp	Sesame seeds (crushed)	
1 tblsp	Soya milk	
Pinch	Oregano, basil, borage, mace, cayenne pepper	
	Pastry No. 1 [see page 76]	
	Salt to taste	

Roll pastry thickly on lightly floured board, cut into 4 inch squares. Heat oil in pan and simmer onion until transparent. Stir rest of ingredients (except soya milk and mixed vegetables) together and simmer for 5 mins. Put mixture into half the squares, fold over, damp edges with little water. Brush with soya milk, put mini-rolls on well oiled baking sheet and bake for 10-15 mins or fry in hot margarine, browning both sides.

200° electric 400°F Gas Mark 6 Near top

Lightly poach mixed vegetables in large shallow pan with a little water. Season with salt, cover with lid for about 5 mins. Transfer vegetables to warm dish and serve with mini-rolls and mashed potato.

POTATO AND SPINACH ENVELOPES

1 lb	Spinach (washed)	(450g)
1	Small onion (peeled & minced)	
2	Mushrooms (chopped)	
2	Small tomatoes	
1 tblsp	Pumpkin seeds (crushed)	
8 oz	Potato (cooked & mashed)	(1 cup - 225g)
2 tblsp	Soya milk	
1 tblsp	Sunflower oil	
Pinch	Sesame seeds (crushed), mace, cayenne pepper	
	Pastry No. 1 [see page 76]	
	Salt to taste	

Put spinach in pan with just enough water to cover bottom, simmer gently, pressing leaves down, for 5 mins. Drain in colander, pressing out surplus liquid, then mince. Heat oil and simmer onion until transparent. Mix with spinach, pumpkin seeds, mushroom, soya milk, herbs and half the potato. Roll out pastry and cut into 5 inch squares. Spread spinach mixture over one half of each square, fold over and damp edges with little water. Brush with milk. Season with salt. Put on baking sheet and bake for about 15 mins or until brown.

200° electric 400°F Gas Mark 6 Near top

Pipe rest of potato into rosettes with an icing bag on to an oiled sheet and brown under grill. Serve with slices of tomato.

CONTINENTAL QUICHE

8 oz	Chopped vegetables in season, such as Mushrooms, tomatoes, parsnip, cucumber, red or green sweet pepper (deseeded)	(2 cups - 225g)
1	Onion (chopped & lightly browned in sunflower oil)	
4 oz	Potato (mashed)	(1½ cups - 300 ml)
6 oz	Water or vegetable stock	(1¼ cups - 175 ml)
1 teasp	Potato flour	
1 clove	Garlic (peeled & crushed) [optional]	
¼ teasp	Ground ginger	
½ teasp	Turmeric	
1 tblsp	Sunflower or soya oil	
1	Bay leaf	
½ teasp	Chives (chopped)	
	Salt & pepper to taste	

Lightly brown onion in oil in shallow pan and then add other ingredients, except potato. Bring to boil and simmer for 5 mins. Sprinkle potato flour over mixture and stir gently for another 5 mins. Remove bay leaf, then place in heat proof dish, pipe with mashed potato. Dot with margarine and brown under grill.

QUICK TANGY HOTPOT

12 oz	Mixed vegetables, such as Tomato, carrot, stick of celery, ½ sweet red pepper (deseeded & chopped), onion, small swede, mushrooms)	(3 cups - 350g)
1 clove	Garlic (chopped)	
6 oz	Water	(¾ cup - 175ml)
1 teasp	Curry powder	
¼ teasp	Allspice	
2 tblsp [heaped]	Dates (chopped)	

1 teasp	Rice flour
Pinch	Paprika
	Salt & pepper to taste

Lightly brown onion in sunflower or soya oil, add rest of vegetables, finely chopped. Cook for 7 mins, then add rest of ingredients, cooking for a further 3 mins. Serve with rice or a jacket potato.

RICE WITH BANANA FRITTERS

4 tblsp	Rice	(1 cup - 95g)
4	Small bananas	
½	Red pepper (washed, deseeded & chopped)	
4	Large mushrooms (chopped)	
1 tblsp	Sultanas	
1 tblsp	Walnuts (chopped)	
8 oz	Sunflower oil	(1 cup - 225ml)
Pinch	Turmeric, nutmeg	
	Batter	
	Salt to taste	
	Alfalfa for garnishing	

Cover sultanas in saucepan with water and simmer until they resemble grapes. Drain and keep warm in oven. Heat a little oil and simmer mushrooms and pepper until soft. Mix with sultanas. Cover rice in saucepan with water and boil gently for 12 mins until rice is soft, add turmeric and season with salt. Drain and mix with mushrooms and sultanas. Slice bananas lengthwise and dip in batter. Carefully put into hot oil and turn until brown all over. Serve on rice. Sprinkle a little nutmeg over each banana, add walnuts and garnish with alfalfa.

MIXED SALAD WITH FRUIT

1	Lettuce (washed & thinly sliced)
1	Eating apple (peeled, cored & sliced)
2	Tomatoes (washed & sliced)
1	Small red pepper (washed, deseeded & sliced)
½	Cucumber (washed & sliced into rings)
1	Clementine orange (sectioned)
Few	Walnuts, dates (stoned)
2 tblsp	Fructose
	Juice of 1 Lemon
	Salad dressing [see page 70]
	Salt to taste

Put orange sections on plate and sprinkle with Fructose, leave aside for a couple of hours to marinate. Put lettuce on large plate. Mix walnuts with salad dressing and put in centre of lettuce. Arrange cucumber rings around dressing, then dates and tomatoes. Dip apple slices in lemon juice to prevent browning and stand these upright round dressing. Remove oranges, shaking off excess Fructose, and arrange round outside of plate. Season tomatoes and cucumber with salt and, lastly, put slices of red pepper round edge of dish.

SAVORY CABBAGE ROLLS

2 oz	Blackeye beans (soaked overnight)	(1 cup - 50g)
4 oz	Mushroom (chopped)	(1 cup - 100g)
¼	Red pepper (washed, deseeded & chopped)	
1	Onion (peeled & chopped)	
8	Cabbage leaves (washed)	
1 handful	Bean sprouts	
2 tblsp	Sunflower oil	
1 tblsp	Soya milk	
2 teasp	Onion seeds	
1 teasp	Mustard seeds	
Pinch	Oregano, basil	

Salt to taste

Cover beans in saucepan with water, bring to boil, reduce heat and simmer for ½ hour. Drain and mix with onion, pepper, mushroom, mustard, salt and herbs. Put 2 cabbage leaves together and spoon bean mixture equally over the 4 leaf pairs. Roll them and put in well oiled casserole. Cover bottom of dish with a little water. Dot each with milk and bake for 25 mins.

190° electric 375°F Gas Mark 5   Near top

Put bean sprouts in heated oil, add onion seeds, stir round for 5 mins and serve with cabbage rolls.

SPICED SAVORY LOAF

4 oz	Butter beans (soaked overnight) (1 cup - 100g)	
1 tblsp	Tapioca (cover with boiling water & stand for 1 hour before use)	
1 tblsp	Sunflower or soya oil	
4 oz	Breadcrumbs	(1 cup - 100g)
2	Tomatoes (sliced)	
1 clove	Garlic (skinned & chopped)	
1	Onion (peeled & chopped)	
4 oz	Potato (mashed)	
1	Sweet red or green pepper (deseeded & chopped)	
1 teasp	Curry powder	
Pinch	Ginger	
	Salt & pepper to taste	

Lightly fry onion in oil. Combine all ingredients in a bowl and mix well. Empty into well oiled 1lb bread tin and bake for 1 hour.

190° electric   375°F Gas Mark 5 Just above centre

SAVORY RICE CAKES

8 oz	Pudding rice (cooked)	(1¼ cups - 225g)
2 oz	Butter beans (soaked overnight)	(¼ cup - 50g)
2 tblsp	Tapioca gel [see recipe page 74]	
2 tblsp	Sunflower or soya oil	
1 teasp	Curry powder	
Sprig	Parsley (chopped)	
	Small quantity of rice flour	
	Salt & pepper to taste	

Mix rice and tapioca gel; stir well. Add salt. Drain water, cover beans with fresh water, bring to boil, reduce heat and simmer for ½ hour. Puree in food processor or mince finely with rice. Thicken with a little rice flour and stir well. Shape into cakes and fry in oil for about 10 mins or until brown on both sides. Makes 6 cakes.

SWEET POTATO, RAISIN AND NUT PIE

	Pastry No. 1 [see page 76]	
2	Medium sweet potatoes (peeled & diced)	
½	Green pepper (washed, deseeded & chopped)	
1 tblsp	Raisins	
1 tblsp	Sunflower oil	
1 tblsp	Lemon juice	
1 tblsp	Hazelnuts	
1 teasp	Curry powder	
1 teasp	Chives (chopped)	
Pinch	Cayenne pepper	
	Salt to taste	

Oil 7 inch flan dish, line with pastry. Put sweet potatoes in pan, cover with water, bring to boil, reduce heat and simmer for 10 mins. Drain and mash, put into bowl and add curry powder, cayenne and chives. Put raisins in saucepan, bring to boil, reduce heat and simmer for 15 mins or until they resemble

grapes. Add salt. drain and mix with sweet potato and lemon
juice. Heat oil and simmer green pepper for few minutes, then
mix with sweet potato. Spoon mixture into pie case. Sprinkle
with nuts and bake for 25 mins or until brown. Garnish with
watercress.
190° electric   375°F Gas Mark 5 Just above centre

STUFFED TOMATOES
SERVED WITH POTATO CROQUETTES

1 tblsp	Lentils (soaked overnight)
1	Onion (peeled & chopped)
4	Large tomatoes (depipped & centres removed)
2	Large mushrooms (chopped)
1 clove	Garlic (skinned & crushed)
2	Large potatoes (peeled & diced)
1 tblsp	Sunflower oil
2 tblsp	Soya milk
1 tblsp	Breadcrumbs (home-made)
1 tblsp	Margarine
Pinch	Chives, basil, marjoram
	Salt to taste
	Watercress for garnishing

Boil lentils in pan with water, then simmer for ¾ hour. Drain
and mince or put through coffee grinder. Put in bowl, mix in
herbs, garlic and mushroom. Spoon mixture into tomatoes, dot
with margarine, season with salt and bake for 20 mins.
180° electric   400°F Gas Mark 5   Near top

CROQUETTES:
Boil potatoes, reduce heat and simmer for 15 mins. Drain,
mash finely, add little milk and mix well. Season with salt. Roll
into sausage shapes, put croquettes in and bake for 20 mins, dip
in soya milk, roll in breadcrumbs, oil a casserole dish and
brown under grill. Garnish with watercress
200° electric   400°F Gas Mark 6   Near top

SAVORY RINGS

4 oz	Plain flour	(1 cup - 100g)
1 oz	Margarine	(1 tblsp- 25g)
2 teasp	Baking powder	
4 tblsp	Soya milk	
Pinch	Paprika, sage, marjoram	
	Salt & pepper to taste	

Mix all dry ingredients well, then rub in margarine until it resembles crumbs, then add soya milk. Roll out about ¼ inch thick on floured board. Cut into rings. Place round top of casseroles and stews when nearly cooked. Put back into oven and bake for a further 15 mins.

200° electric   400°F Gas Mark 6   Top of oven

SPINACH FLAN

2 oz	Butter beans (soaked overnight)	(2 heaped tblsp - 50g)
16 oz	Fresh spinach	(2 cups - 460g)
16 oz	Potato (mashed)	(2 cups - 460g)
1 tblsp	Margarine	
5 slices	Sweet pepper	
Pinch	Nutmeg, mint	
Little	Parsley	
	Salt & pepper to taste	

Drain beans and cover with fresh water, add salt and pepper. Bring to boil, reduce heat and simmer for 20 mins. Drain off water and purée in food processor or mince. Oil a 1lb bread tin, put beans on bottom. Put spinach in saucepan with a little water. Add condiments and cook with covered lid for 5 mins. Drain water, spread spinach on beans, sprinkle with nutmeg and mint. Cover with mashed potato. Lay slices of pepper on top and dot all over with margarine. Bake for 20 mins.

190° electric   375°F Gas Mark 4   Just above centre
Garnish with parsley.

SAVORY SPINACH CRÊPES

| 1 lb | Fresh spinach (washed) | (450g) |
| 1 | Onion (finely chopped) | |

Remove spinach stalks. Cook in just enough water to cover the bottom of a saucepan. Drain and squeeze until spinach appears quite dry. Fry onion until transparent in a little sunflower oil. Add salt and pepper to taste and leave in warm oven.

PASTRY:
9 oz	Self raising flour	(2½ cups - 250g)
3 oz	Margarine	(⅓ cup - 75g)
Pinch	Nutmeg	
Little	Water	

Add enough water to flour to make a stiff dough and roll on to floured board. Cut into 5 inch rounds. Fry pancakes 3 mins each side. Spread spinach and a little onion into each pancake. Fold in half. Spread margarine on top of each pancake. Arrange on fireproof dish or pan. Place under grill until margarine is melted. Serve immediately. Makes 4 crêpes.

SAVORY NUT CROQUETS

4 oz	Butter beans (soaked overnight) (¼ cup - 125g)
1	Medium onion (peeled & chopped)
1 teasp	Tapioca (soaked 1 hour in boiling water)
1 teasp [heaped]	Nuts (chopped)
1 teasp	Chives (chopped)
3 tblsp	Sunflower or soya oil
4 tblsp	Breadcrumbs (home-made)
1 clove	Garlic (skinned & chopped)
½ teasp	Mixed spice
Pinch	Cayenne pepper
	Salt to taste

Drain, then cover beans with fresh water, bring to boil, reduce heat, add salt and pepper and simmer for ½ hour. Drain off water and puree in food processor or mince. Lightly fry onion in oil. Blend all ingredients, except oil and breadcrumbs. Mix well, roll into sausage shapes and roll in breadcrumbs. Heat oil in frying pan and brown croquets all over for about 10 mins.

CHINESE STIR FRY

1 tblsp	Sunflower oil	
1 teasp	Potato flour	
¼ pt	Water	(⅔ cup - 150ml)
1 clove	Garlic (skinned & chopped)	
1	Large onion (peeled & chopped)	
1	Medium potato (peeled & sliced)	
1 tblsp	Cashew nuts (chopped)	
2 tblsp	Frozen peas	
2 tblsp	Frozen sweet corn	
2	Mushrooms (washed & chopped)	
2 oz	Mange-tout peas (washed)	
Pinch	Chinese 5-spice, cayenne pepper	
	Salt & pepper to taste	

Lightly fry onion in a shallow pan. Add mange-tout peas with water for 5 mins. Add rest of ingredients and simmer for further 3 mins. Serve with rice

SPICED SUPPER DISH

4 oz	Mixed frozen vegetables	(¾ cup - 125g)
1 tblsp	Sunflower or soya oil	
1	Large onion (peeled & chopped)	
4 oz	Mushrooms	(¾ cup - 125g)
½ pt	Water	(1¼ cups - 300ml)
½	Red pepper (deseeded & chopped)	
1 clove	Garlic (skinned & chopped)	
1 teasp	Fructose	

1 teasp	Rice flour
2	Medium tomatoes (blanched & deseeded)
1	Pear (peeled, cored & sliced)
Pinch	Ginger, paprika, cayenne pepper
	Salt & pepper to taste

Lightly fry onion in oil. Add all other ingredients. Bring to boil, reduce heat and simmer for 5 mins. Serve with mashed potato.

CURRY WITH BANANAS

½ pt	Water	(1¼ cups - 300ml)
1	Onion (peeled & chopped)	
2	Tomatoes (deseeded & chopped)	
2 tblsp	Peas	
1 teasp	Curry powder	
1 tblsp	Sunflower or soya oil	
1	Small apple (peeled, cored & chopped)	
1	Small potato (peeled & chopped)	
1	Carrot (chopped)	
1	Parsnip (peeled & chopped)	
1 teasp	Potato flour	
1	Banana (skinned & sliced lengthwise)	
1 teasp	Fructose	

Brown onion in oil in shallow pan. Add other ingredients, except potato flour and banana. Bring to boil, reduce heat and simmer for 5 mins. Sprinkle flour over top. Stir for another minute. Remove from heat. Brown banana strip in margarine. Serve curry mixture with rice, placing banana on top.

BEAN AND POTATO SAVORY CAKES

3 oz	Butter beans (soaked overnight)	(¼ cup - 75 g)
2 oz	Breadcrumbs	(½ cup - 50g)
2 oz	Plain flour	(1 cup - 50g)
2 teasp	Tapioca (soaked in boiling water for 1 hour)	
½ teasp	Mixed herbs	
2 tblsp	Sunflower or soya oil	
1	Small onion (peeled & chopped)	
6 oz	Potato (mashed)	(½ cup - 175g)
	Salt & pepper	

Cover beans with new water, adding condiments to taste. Bring to boil, reduce heat and simmer for ½ hour. Grind beans in food processor or mincer. Lightly fry onion in oil, saving oil. Mix onion and all ingredients together. Shape into cakes and brown on both sides for 10 mins. This makes about 8 cakes.

ROASTED JERUSALEM ARTICHOKES

1lb	Jerusalem artichokes	(450g)
	Salt	
	Sunflower oil	

Thinly peel artichokes and slice into small sections. Heat oil in casserole, adding artichokes. Season and roast for about ¾ hour.

190° electric 375°F Gas Mark 5 Near top

AUBERGINES WITH GARLIC SAUCE

2	Fairly large aubergines (peeled & sliced)
1 tblsp	Sunflower oil
2 cloves	Garlic (skinned & crushed)
1 tblsp	Margarine
Pinch	Turmeric
Good squeeze Lemon	
	Salt

Sprinkle aubergines with salt and leave for ½ hour to draw out excess water. Rinse, then dry. Put in oiled casserole. Put garlic in mixing bowl with oil and margarine (melted). Add turmeric and juice, stir well, then spread all over each slice of aubergine. Bake in oven for 20 mins.

190° electric 375°F Gas Mark 5 Just above centre

BEANS WITH ONION GLAZE

3 tblsp	Mixed dried beans (soaked overnight)
½ pt	Mixed vegetable juice (1¼ cups - 300ml)
1	Large Spanish onion (peeled & sliced)
1 tblsp	Sunflower oil
1 teasp	Onion seeds
	Salt & pepper to taste
	Watercress for garnish

Put beans and juice in casserole. Lightly brown onion in oil, add to beans with rest of ingredients, except watercress. Cover and bake for 1 hour.
  200° electric 400°F Gas Mark 6 Just above centre
Garnish with watercress.

HARICOT BEANS WITH CARROTS

4 oz	Haricot beans (soaked overnight) (¾ cup - 100g)
4 oz	Carrots (washed & sliced)
Pinch	Rosemary, nutmeg, cumin seeds
	Watercress for garnish
	Salt & pepper to taste

Place all ingredients in casserole. Cover and bake 1 hour. Garnish with watercress.
  200° electric 400°F Gas Mark 6   Just above centre

SCARLET RUNNER BEANS

4 oz   Runner beans (stringed & sliced) (¾ cup - 100g)

1 tblsp Sunflower oil
1 teasp Mustard seeds
        Salt & pepper to taste
        Rosehip syrup and watercress to garnish

Heat oil in large shallow pan. Add beans and mustard seeds, cover with lid and cook gently for 5 mins, stirring occasionally to stop burning. Add condiments. Turn into serving dish and garnish with rosehip syrup and watercress.

BROAD BEANS WITH ROSE HIP GLAZE AND SPICES

4 oz   Broad beans (shelled)   (¾ cup - 100g)
1 tblsp   Sunflower oil
1 teasp   Mustard seeds
Pinch   Tarragon, sage
               Salt & pepper to taste
               Rosehip syrup
Small quantity   Alfalfa

Put beans in well oiled casserole, cover bottom with water, add condiments and herbs. Cover. Bake 1 hour. 160° electric 325°F Gas Mark 5 Just above centre Remove from oven, pour rosehip syrup over top and garnish with alfalfa and mustard seeds. This recipe serves one

RUNNER BEANS WITH PARSLEY AND GARLIC

1 lb	Runner beans (sliced thin) (1½ cups - 450g)
1 clove	Garlic (skinned & crushed)
Pinch	Rosemary, tarragon, nutmeg
	Salt & pepper to taste
	Margarine for garnish

Put beans in large shallow pan. Cover with water, season with condiments, cover, bring to boil, then simmer until liquid has evaporated - about 10 mins. Sprinkle herbs over beans. Add garlic and dots of margarine.

BOILED BEETROOT WITH ONION

4	Small beetroot (washed)
1	Large Spanish onion (peeled & chopped)
Pinch	Chives (chopped)
	Salt & pepper to taste
	Margarine for garnish

Cover beetroot with water, boil for 1 hour or so. Cool, rub off skin, dice and put in fireproof dish. Lightly brown onion until transparent and arrange round beetroot. Season with condiments. Dot with margarine and serve at once.

STUFFED BEETROOT

2	Medium sized beetroot (cooked)
2	Small gherkins
2 tblsp	Potato (mashed)
1 tblsp	Parsley (chopped)
1 teasp each of Capers, Chive, Paprika, Grated shallot

| 1 clove | Garlic (skinned & crushed) |
| | Salt & pepper to taste |

Rub off outer skin of beetroot, carefully hollow each out, leaving thin wall. Mix all ingredients (including beetroot scooped from middle), except capers and paprika, and spoon into beetroot shell. Sprinkle with paprika, dot capers on tops and serve immediately.

BROCCOLI AND CARROTS

1 lb	Broccoli heads (washed & sectioned)
	(1½ cups - 450g)
2	Medium carrots (scraped & sliced)
1 tblsp	Sunflower oil
2 tblsp	Water
	Onion seeds
	Salt & pepper to taste
	Margarine for garnish

Gently boil ingredients in large shallow pan for 5 mins or until water covering bottom of pan has evaporated. Add onion seeds, dot with margarine and serve at once.

BRUSSELS SPROUTS AND CARROTS

12	Large Brussels sprouts (washed & sliced)
3	Good sized carrots (washed & thinly sliced)
1 tblsp	Sunflower oil
2 tblsp	Water
	Mustard seeds
	Salt & pepper to taste
	Margarine & paprika for garnish

Pour water into large shallow pan, add carrots and poach for 5 mins with lid on. Add oil, sprouts and

46

condiments. Cook at fairly high heat for further 3 mins, stirring constantly. Sprinkle with mustard seeds, serve at once with paprika and margarine.

BRUSSELS SPROUTS AND LEEKS

12   Large Brussels sprouts (washed & sliced)
2   Medium leeks (washed & sliced thinly)
2 tblsp Water
1 tblsp Sunflower oil
         Onion seeds, basil
         Salt & pepper to taste

Put leeks, sprouts and water into large shallow pan, cover and poach over fairly high heat for about 10 mins or until water has evaporated. Season with condiments. Pour oil over vegetables and stir well. Sprinkle onion seeds and basil over and serve immediately.

CELERY STUFFED WITH POTATO, NUTS AND HERBS

1   Medium celery head (wash, trimmed & sliced
         into 4 inch strips)
6 oz   Potato (mashed)   (1 cup - 175g)
1 tblsp Mixed nuts (chopped)
1 teasp Sesame seeds
1 clove Garlic (skinned & crushed)
Pinch   Mace, caraway seed, mustard seed, paprika
         Salt & pepper to taste
         Margarine for garnish

Boil celery strips until tender, then put on piece of tissue to dry. Mix nuts, sesame seeds and potato well, add rest of ingredients. Stir well again, then pipe potato mixture into each strip of celery. Dot all over with margarine, put under grill until nicely brown. Lastly, sprinkle paprika over each strip.

RED CABBAGE AND APPLE WITH MIXED HERBS

1	Small red cabbage (washed & sliced thinly)
½ pt	Apple juice (1 ¼ cups - 300ml)
1 teasp	Fructose
Pinch	Basil, thyme, nutmeg, parsley (chopped)
Few strips	Orange peel
1	Medium cooking apple (peeled & cored)
Juice of 1 orange	
	Potato flour
	Salt & pepper to taste

Put cabbage and juice in pan, bring to boil, reduce heat and simmer for 15 mins. Add Fructose, basil, thyme and nutmeg. Put apple in saucepan with just enough water to cover bottom of pan, simmer gently, but do not let apples become mushy. Mix orange juice and flour, then add to apple. Gently boil until apple thickens. Spoon cabbage into serving dish, pour apple mixture over top. Put orange strips on top and garnish with parsley.

CABBAGE SLICES WITH ONION GLAZE

1	White cabbage (about 1 lb) (washed & centre removed)
2 tblsp	Sunflower oil
2 tblsp	Water
2 tblsp	Margarine
½	Small red pepper (washed & deseeded)
1	Onion (peeled & sliced)

48

Pinch   Mace
                Salt & pepper to taste
                Sprigs of parsley & paprika for garnishing

Cut cabbage into wafer thin slices. Put in large pan with hot oil. Add onion and red pepper, stirring constantly for a few minutes. Add other ingredients, except margarine. Cover and cook for 10 mins stirring occasionally. Melt margarine and pour over top. Stir thoroughly and put in serving dish, garnishing with parsley and paprika.

CABBAGE ENVELOPES

12   Outer leaves of white cabbage (washed)
4 tblsp Potato (mashed)
4   Tomatoes (washed, chopped & depipped)
Pinch   Mace, oregano, mustard seeds, basil
         Flaked almonds
         Margarine
         Salt & pepper to taste

Dry cabbage leaves and put 3 together slightly overlapping, making 4 envelopes. Into each put 1 tblsp potato, 1 tomato and a pinch of condiment and herbs. Fold each envelope and secure with toothpick or cocktail stick. Put in well oiled casserole, dot all over with margarine. Cover bottom of dish with a little water, cover with lid and bake for 40 mins.
  200° electric 400°F Gas Mark 6 Just above centre
  Sprinkle with almonds

SAUTÉED CABBAGE WITH APPLE AND BEAN SPROUTS

½	Small white cabbage (washed & finely shredded)
1	Small cooking apple (peeled, cored & chopped)
1 handful	Bean sprouts (washed)
1 tblsp	Margarine
1 tblsp	Onion seeds
1 tblsp	Sunflower oil
Pinch	Mace, basil, cumin seeds, paprika
Little	Water
	Salt & pepper to taste

Pour enough water into a large shallow pan to cover bottom. Simmer cabbage for 5 mins. Add bean sprouts and oil and simmer for further 3 mins. Add apple, condiments and herbs and stir well for a couple of minutes. The vegetables should be fairly crisp. Garnish with onion seeds and margarine. Sprinkle paprika on top.

CABBAGE AND PEPPER WITH APRICOT SAUCE

½	Small cabbage (washed & shredded)
1	Red pepper (washed, deseeded & chopped)
4 tblsp	Apricot purée (cooked & sweetened)
1 tblsp	Margarine
I tblsp	Sunflower oil
Little Water	
	Small quantity of basic sauce [page 69]
	Flaked almonds
	Chopped parsley
	Salt & pepper to taste

50

Put cabbage in large shallow pan, the bottom covered with water. Cover and simmer. for 5 mins. Add red pepper and simmer for 3 mins or until water has evaporated. Add margarine, oil and condiments and mix well. Pour basic sauce and purée into saucepan and heat, stirring constantly to prevent burning. Put cabbage into serving dish, pour sauce over top, then sprinkle almonds and parsley round top.

APRICOT PURÉE:
2 tblsp dried apricots boiled in water until soft. Add Fructose to taste, then. cool and put through either sieve or in liquidiser for a few seconds.

CABBAGE PANCAKES WITH APPLE AND ORANGE SAUCE

	Pastry No. 1 [see page 76]
½	Small white cabbage (washed & shredded)
2 teasp	Potato flour
1	Cooking apple (peeled, cored & chopped)
1 teasp	Nuts (chopped)
Pinch	Mace, cumin seed, ginger
	Juice of 1 small orange
	Salt & pepper to taste

Roll pastry out on light!y floured board and cut into four 5 inch squares. Put cabbage and apple into a shallow pan, cover bottom with little water, cover and simmer for 5 mins or until all water has evaporated. Add herbs and condiments. Stir well and cook for further 5 mins. Oil casserole, divide the mixture equally into each pastry square, leaving about ½ inch all round to seal edge. Fold each square over and seal with water. Put pancakes into casserole. Cover and bake for 40 mins.

200° electric 400°F Gas Mark 6 Just above centre

APPLE AND ORANGE SAUCE:
Simmer apple and orange juice together with ¼ pint
water. Sweeten to taste. Thicken with 2 teasp potato
flour and 1 tblsp water. Pour over pancakes. Garnish
with nuts.

CASSEROLE OF MIXED VEGETABLES

1	Green pepper (washed, deseeded & chopped)	
1	Leek (washed & trimmed!	
2	Large tomatoes (blanched, skin & pips removed)	
1 clove	Garlic (skinned & chopped)	
1 tblsp	Broad beans (soaked overnight)	(2 cups - 100g)
4 oz	Bamboo shoots	(2 cups - 100g)
4 oz	Mushrooms	(1 cup - 100g)
4 oz	Bean sprouts	(2 cups - 100g)
Pinch	Borage, basil, oregano	
	Salt & pepper to taste	

Put all ingredients into well greased casserole, cover
and bake for 45 mins
200° electric   400°F Gas Mark 6   Just above
centre

CORNISH PASTY

	Pastry No. 1 [see page 76]
1	Medium potato (peeled & diced)
2 tblsp	Green peas
1	Small onion (peeled. & chopped)
	Carrot (scraped & diced)
	Salt & pepper to taste

Roll pastry on lightly floured board and divide into 5 inch squares. Mix other ingredients and spoon equal quantities into each square, dampen edges of pastry and seal. Bake on well oiled baking sheet for 45 mins, covering with foil to prevent burning.

200° electric   400°F Gas Mark 6   Near oven top

CAULIFLOWER AND CHESTNUT SAUCE

1	Medium cauliflower (cut into florets)
4 oz	Chestnuts (boiled & minced) (1 cup - 100g)
1	Onion (peeled & chopped)
Pinch	Rosemary
	Basic sauce [see page 69]
	Salt & pepper to taste

Put cauliflower, onion, condiments and herb in well greased casserole. Mix chestnuts in sauce, then pour over cauliflower. Bake for 1 hour or until cooked.

200" electric   400°F Gas Mark 6   Near oven top

STUFFED COURGETTES

4	Medium courgettes (washed)
2	Large mushrooms (chopped)
¾ teasp	Mixed herbs
Pinch	Chives, cayenne pepper
Little	Sunflower oil
	Salt to taste

Cut a wedge lengthwise from each courgette, scoop out flesh, reserve shells, season flesh with salt. Gently fry mushroom in oil until lightly brown and soft. Add all ingredients to courgette flesh. Spoon mixture back into shells, put in oiled casserole and bake for 45 mins.

180° electric   350°F Gas Mark 5   Near oven top

CELERY PURÉE

1   Celery heart (washed, outer leaves removed)
2 heaped teasp Potato flour
1 teasp Lemon juice
1 teasp Mustard seeds
         Salt & pepper to taste

Mince celery finely, put in saucepan, cover with water and season with salt. Boil gently for 10 mins, stirring to stop sticking, turn down heat and simmer for 5 mins. Add juice and mustard. Thicken with flour mixed with little water to thick paste. Bring to boil, then stir until it thickens. Cool, then put through sieve.

CELERIAC WITH PINEAPPLE AND SULTANAS

1   Celeriac (washed & trimmed)
2 tblsp   Sultanas (washed)
1 tblsp   Flaked almonds
1 small tin Pineapple pieces
             Potato flour for thickening
             Salt & pepper to taste

Slice celeriac thinly into saucepan, season with salt, cover with water and boil gently for 10 mins. Remove celeriac and use water to boil sultanas until they appear plump like baby grapes. Remove from heat, drain off excess liquid and add pineapple juice. Thicken with flour mixed to a paste with a little of the juice. Bring to boil, reduce heat and stir constantly until it thickens. Oil a casserole, put celeriac over bottom, then spoon sauce on top. Sprinkle almonds and bake for 30 mins.
        180° electric   350° Gas Mark 5 Centre oven

CURRIED VEGETABLES

1 tblsp	Butter beans (soaked overnight)
1 each	Leek, onion, carrot, small swede, potato, small cauliflower, small red pepper
1 clove	Garlic (skinned & crushed)
¼ teasp	Ground ginger
½ teasp	Coriander seeds, cumin seeds (both crushed), oregano, borage
6 oz	Patna rice

Wash and prepare all vegetables and put in pan, adding water to halfway up pan. Stir in rest of ingredients, except rice, season with condiments. Bring to boil, reduce heat and simmer for 30 mins or until done.
Serve with boiled rice: Cook rice in large saucepan with salt seasoned water for 12 mins. Drain. Turn on to large dish and pour mixed vegetables into centre.

DANDELION ENVELOPES

	Large bunch Dandelion leaves
	Pastry No. 1 [see page 76]
	Little Fructose
Pinch	Mace
1 teasp	Lemon juice
	Salt & pepper to taste

Roll pastry on floured board, cut into four 5 inch squares and leave in cool place. Put dandelion leaves and juice in pan over low heat, covered, until leaves have shrunk down. Add condiments. Cook for a further few minutes until all liquid has evaporated. Spoon dandelion into each square, seal edges of pastry with water. Put on baking sheet and bake for 30 mins.
190° electric 375° F Gas Mark 5 Near top

LEEKS AND CARROTS

2   Medium sized leeks (washed & trimmed)
2   Medium sized carrots (scraped & sliced)
1 tblsp Sunflower oil
1 teasp Margarine
Pinch   Onion seeds, marjoram, oregano
Few sprigs Parsley
        Salt & pepper to taste

Heat oil in large shallow pan. Put in vegetables, cover and simmer for 10 mins, stirring occasionally to stop burning. Add other ingredients, except margarine and parsley. Stir for few minutes. Serve immediately, garnished with parsley and margarine.

LEEKS AND OLIVES WITH PINEAPPLE SAUCE

2   Medium sized leeks (washed & trimmed)
1 heaped tblsp Black olives (stoned)
1 teasp   Potato flour
¾ pt   Pineapple juice   (2 cups - 150ml)
Pinch   Tarragon
Few   Flaked almonds
            Salt & pepper to taste

Slice leeks into thin rings and put in large shallow pan. Season with salt, add enough water to cover pan bottom. Cover, then simmer, stirring occasionally. Add olives, tarragon and juice, mix well. Add flour mixed with little water into thick paste. Stir into vegetables until mixture thickens. Serve immediately

LETTUCE AND ONIONS WITH BEAN SPROUTS

12	Outer lettuce leaves (washed & sliced)
2	Medium onions (peeled & chopped)
1 handful	Bean sprouts (washed)
1 tblsp	Sunflower oil
1 teasp	Onion seeds
	Salt & Pepper to taste

Heat oil in large shallow pan, simmer onion until golden brown. Add bean sprouts and condiments, mix well. Lastly add lettuce and onion seeds. Stir until leaves are shrunk and limp. Serve immediately.

STUFFED MUSHROOMS WITH GARLIC AND PEPPER

3	Large mushrooms
1	Medium green pepper (deseeded & chopped)
½	Red pepper (deseeded & chopped)
1	Small onion (peeled & chopped)
1 clove	Garlic (skinned & crushed)
1 tblsp	Butter beans (soaked overnight)
1 tblsp	Sunflower oil
1 tblsp	Margarine
1 tblsp	Lemon juice
1 teasp	Fructose
	Salt to taste
	Parsley or alfalfa for garnishing

Cover beans with fresh water and boil gently for ½ hour. Drain and mince finely. Lightly brown peppers and onion in oil. Mix them and juice, garlic, Fructose and salt with the beans. Dot margarine over mushrooms and lightly brown under grill, meanwhile put bean mixture in sauce pan and simmer for 3 mins. Spoon into each mushroom and serve immediately.

ROASTED PARSNIPS

1	Large parsnip (peeled & sectioned)
¾ tblsp	Sunflower oil
	Salt to taste

Boil parsnip in water for 7 mins. Heat oil in casserole, drain parsnip, dry and put in casserole for about 30 mins or until brown.

200° electric   400°F Gas Mark 6   Near top

GLAZED PARSNIPS AND CARROTS

1	Medium parsnip (peeled & sectioned)
2	Large carrots (scraped & sectioned)
1 tblsp	Margarine
Pinch	Rosemary, tarragon, paprika
	Salt to taste

Put vegetables in pan with a little water, salt and herbs. Bring to boil, reduce heat and simmer for 15 mins. Drain and serve with margarine.

MASHED PARSNIP FRITTERS WITH ALFALFA

1	Medium parsnip (peeled & sectioned)
	Batter
2 tblsp	Margarine
Handful	Alfalfa (washed)
Pinch	Tarragon, Pepper
	Sunflower oil for frying
	Salt to taste

Put parsnip in pan of boiling water, season with salt and simmer for about 10 mins. Drain and mash. Mix in tarragon and pepper. Roll into small balls, dip in batter and brown in oil. Serve on a bed of alfalfa.

ONIONS STUFFED WITH MUSHROOMS

2   Large Spanish onions (peeled & par-boiled)
3 tblsp Mushrooms (minced)
1 teasp Onion seeds
1 tblsp Margarine
Pinch   Tarragon
        Salt & pepper to taste

Cover onions with water in pan, boil, reduce heat and simmer for 15 mins. Remove centre of each onion and mince. Add this to the mushroom, sprinkle in onion seeds and tarragon. Mix well, then spoon mixture into onions shells. Wrap onions in foil halfway up, put in greased casserole and bake for 20 mins.
200° electric   400°F Gas Mark 6   Just above centre

ODDS AND ENDS CASSEROLE

1 tblsp   Blackeye beans (soaked overnight)
1 each   Carrot, potato, onion, swede (peeled & chopped)
1 tblsp   Mushroom (chopped)
1   Large tomato (washed & quartered)
1 teasp   Mustard seeds
1 bunch   Watercress
Pinch   Oregano, basil, marjoram
1 handful   Alfalfa (washed)

Put all ingredients in well oiled casserole, cover and

bake for 1 hour.
200° electric   400°F Gas Mark 6   Centre

PETITE MIXED VEGETABLES

6	Button mushrooms (chopped)
6	Spring onions (peeled & chopped)
1 tblsp	Broad beans (soaked overnight)
3 tblsp	Peas
1	Potato (peeled & sliced)
1	Small red pepper (washed, deseeded & chopped)
8 oz	Vegetable juice (1 cup - 225ml)
Little	Allspice
	Salt & pepper to taste

Put all ingredients in oiled casserole. Cover. Bake for
¾ hour.
190° electric   375° F Gas Mark 5   Centre

POTATO AND PEA CROQUETTES

2	Fairly large potatoes (peeled & chopped)
4 tblsp	Peas
2 tblsp	Soya milk
4 tblsp	Home-made breadcrumbs
1 teasp	Orange peel (grated)
Pinch	Mace, fennel, cayenne pepper
	Salt to taste

Boil potatoes 15 mins, drain and mash. Cook and mash
peas. Mix potatoes, peas, herbs and salt together.
Mould into mini-rolls, cover with milk and roll in
breadcrumbs. Put croquettes into well oiled casserole
and bake for ½ hour.
200° electric 400°F Gas Mark 6   Just above centre

POTATO AND TURNIP SNOWBALLS

2   Medium sized potatoes (peeled & chopped)
1   Small turnip (peeled & chopped)
1 teasp Curry powder
1 tblsp Lemon juice
2 tblsp Soya milk
Pinch Ginger, mace
       Salt to taste

Boil potato and turnip for 15 mins. Drain and mash, add salt, curry powder, herbs and juice. Mix well and shape into balls, dip in soya milk, then put in well oiled casserole and bake for ½ hour.

     200° electric   400°F Gas Mark 6   Centre

POTATO CAKES

2   Large potatoes (peeled & chopped)
2 tblsp Potato flour
3 tblsp Soya milk
Pinch Mace, chives
       Salt to taste

Boil potato for 15 mins. Drain and mash to fine cream, add herbs and a little soya milk, mix well. Season with salt towards end of cooking. Shape into cakes, dip in little soya milk and roll in potato flour. Put in well oiled casserole and bake for ½ hour.

     200° electric   400°F Gas Mark 6   Near top

POTATO AND SPINACH CAKES

2	Medium potatoes (peeled & chopped)	
1 lb	Spinach (washed)	(450g)
2 tblsp	Soya milk	
1 tblsp	Potato flour	
1 clove	Garlic (skinned & crushed)	
Few sprigs	Parsley	
	Salt, marjoram, nutmeg, pepper to taste	

Boil potatoes for 15 mins, then spinach for 5 mins in same water. Liquidise spinach and mash potatoes. Add herbs and salt. Shape into cakes, dip in soya milk, roll in flour, put in well oiled casserole for ½ hour.

200° electric   400°F Gas Mark 6   Near top
Garnish with parsley.

POTATO PIE WITH SUNFLOWER SEEDS

	Pastry No. 1 [see page 76]	
1	Medium sized onion (peeled & sliced)	
1	Large potato (peeled & grated)	
1 tblsp	Sunflower seeds (crushed)	
1 tblsp ∨	Margarine	
1 teasp	Lemon juice	
Pinch	Borage, chives	
	Salt & pepper to taste	
	Parsley for garnishing	

Line well oiled 7 inch flan tin with pastry, put onion and juice on bottom, then potato, herbs and condiments. Sprinkle sunflower seeds over top and dot with margarine. Cover and bake for 30 mins.

230° electric   450°F Gas Mark 8   Near top

RATATOUILLE

2	Courgettes (washed & sliced into rings)
1	Small red and green pepper (deseeded & sliced)
1	Medium onion (peeled & sliced)
1	Small aubergine (washed & sliced into rings)
2	Tomatoes (blanched, skinned & halved)
1	Medium potato (peeled & sliced into rings)
2 tblsp	Sunflower oil
1 clove	Garlic (peeled & crushed)
	Salt & pepper to taste

Spread courgettes and aubergines on plate and sprinkle with salt to draw out liquid. After 1 hour wash, then put in well oiled casserole. Heat oil in pan and lightly fry onion until transparent. Put all ingredients in casserole. Cover and bake for 1 hour.

180° electric   350°F Gas Mark 5   Just above
centre

RAINBOW MIXED PLATTER

1	Small lettuce (washed & shredded)	
1	Small orange (peeled & sliced into rings)	
1	Large potato (previously cooked)	
2	Tomatoes (washed & sliced)	
1	Beetroot (cooked & diced)	
1 teasp	Chives (chopped)	
1 tblsp	Nuts (chopped)	
Small	Cucumber (washed & sliced)	
1 tblsp	Fructose	
1 bunch	Radishes (washed & sliced)	
1 6oz tin	Soya cream	(½ cup - 169ml)
Few	Black olives (stoned)	
	Salt & paprika to taste	

Arrange lettuce round large plate. Sprinkle Fructose over orange rings and leave until last. Pour excess whey off tin of soya cream and season with salt, pepper and chives. Mash potato, add half cream and spoon into centre of lettuce, sprinkling a little paprika on top. Arrange beetroot and cucumber around potato, then a circle of radishes outside. Sprinkle nuts over potato salad and arrange slices of olive around edge of plate. Lastly, put orange rings between olives. Serve with rest of soya cream.

SPINACH AND NOODLES ITALIANE

	Pastry No. 1 [see page 76]	
8 oz	Cooked spinach	(1 cup - 225g)
1 tblsp	Sunflower oil	
2 tblsp	Soya milk	
1 teasp	Margarine	
6 oz	Sunflower oil	(1 cup - 175ml)
Little	Mace, paprika	
	Salt to taste	

Season cooked spinach with salt, add mace. Chop finely, then dot margarine over. Leave in warm oven. To make NOODLES: roll out pastry, cut into long strips; roll these into twists, dip in milk and brown in hot oil. Arrange noodles on dish with spinach and serve immediately.

SPINACH AND POTATO GÂTEAU

8 oz	Spinach (previously cooked)	(1 cup - 225g)
1 clove	Garlic (skinned & crushed)	
2	Large potatoes (cooked & mashed)	
1 tblsp	Margarine	
Few sprigs Parsley		

Salt, pepper, cayenne pepper, paprika to taste

Either sieve spinach or put in liquidiser for few seconds. Add salt, pepper and garlic. Blend well. Oil casserole and put spinach over bottom, then a layer of potato. Repeat, ending with a top layer of potato, over which sprinkle cayenne and paprika. Dot margarine over top and bake 30 mins. Finish under grill.
200° electric 400°F Gas Mark 6 Near top
Garnish with parsley.

POACHED SPINACH

Large bunch	Spinach
1	Medium tomato
1 tblsp	Margarine
Little	Mace, sesame seeds (crushed), marjoram
	Salt to taste

Put spinach in fairly large pan, just cover with water, season with salt and poach with lid on for 5 mins. Strain through colander. Sprinkle with little marjoram and mace, dot with margarine. Grill tomato, arrange on top of spinach, garnish with sesame seeds and serve immediately.

STUFFED TOMATOES

4	Large tomatoes (blanched & skinned)
1	Avocado pear (stone & flesh removed)
1 clove	Garlic (skinned & crushed)
1 teasp	Ground almonds
Little	Lemon juice
Pinch	Chives (chopped)
Sprigs	Parsley or Watercress

Slice top off each tomato and scoop out centre and seeds. Wrap each in foil halfway up and chill. Discard stone and skin of avocado and mash flesh with chives. Spoon mixture into each tomato, sprinkle with ground almonds over top and garnish with parsley or watercress.

VEGETABLE BRUNCH

2oz each	Broccoli spears, bean sprouts, cauliflower florets, tomato, leek (½ cup - 50g)
1 teasp	Onion seeds
1 tblsp	Sunflower oil
1 tblsp	Water
Juice	1 lemon
Pinch	Nutmeg, salt, pepper
Little	Margarine

Prepare vegetables, cutting into small sections and put all, except bean sprouts and tomato, in shallow pan with oil. Blanch tomato and remove skin and pips. Chop and add to other ingredients, then add bean sprouts. Cover and cook for 10 mins, turning occasionally. Vegetables should be crisp and fresh looking. Dot with margarine.

VEGETABLE PIE

2 carrots, 2 tomatoes, 1 onion, 1 small swede, 2 sticks celery (all washed, prepared & chopped)

4	Large mushrooms (chopped)
1 clove	Garlic (skinned & crushed)
8 oz	Mixed vegetable juice (1 cup - 225ml)
8 oz	Potato (cooked & mashed) (1 cup - 225g)
Pinch	Oregano, basil, borage, coriander seeds, paprika

Few sprigs Parsley
          Salt to taste

Put all ingredients, except potato, in well oiled casserole. Cover and bake for ¾ to 1 hour or till done.
    190° electric   375°F Gas Mark 5   Centre
Put potato over top, brown under grill. Garnish with parsley.

VEGETABLE ROLY-POLY

	Pastry No. 2 [see page 77]
2	Large mushrooms (minced)
1	Onion (peeled & minced)
1	Small potato (peeled & minced)
1	Carrot (scraped & minced)
1 clove	Garlic (skinned & minced)
2 tblsp	Peas
1 tblsp	Soya milk
	Salt to taste

Roll out pastry to 12 x 7 inches on floured board. Mix other ingredients, except milk, in bowl. Spread over pastry. Seal edges with water, roll, brush all over with soya milk. Roll pastry in greaseproof paper and tie very loosely, leaving space between pastry and paper. Finally, roll in foil and tie edges. Steam for 2 hours in a pan with enough water to just cover roly-poly.

SAUCES, PASTRY and MISCELLANEOUS

APPLE JELLY

Cooking apples in season
Fructose
Lemon juice

Peel and core apples. Put in preserving pan or large saucepan. Cover with water and bring to boil, reduce heat and simmer until apples are soft - about 1 hour. Strain through jelly bags or butter muslin, perhaps leaving overnight. To every pint of juice add 1 lb Fructose (2 cups - 450g) and 3 tblsp lemon juice. Pour juice in preserving pan, bring to boil, add Fructose and boil rapidly until setting point is reached. To test if jelly is set, pour a little off a wooden spoon on to a plate: if the jelly crinkles it is ready. Remove from heat and bottle in clean jars. Place wax disc over each jar and seal with lid or pot covers.

BANANA CREAM

1	Small banana
1 teasp	Fructose
	Enough pineapple juice to cover banana

Slice banana, place in liquidiser with juice and Fructose for a few seconds, until it is like thick cream. Pour over cereal or other fruit. THIS WILL NOT KEEP.

BARBECUE SAUCE

2 tblsp	Sunflower oil
½ pt	Water (1¼ cups - 300ml)
1	Onion (peeled & chopped)
2 tblsp	Mushrooms (chopped)
4 tblsp	Tomato purée [see page 75]
2 tblsp	Fructose
¼ teasp	Mustard seed
½ teasp	Salt & pepper
	Bay leaf
1 tblsp	Potato flour
1 teasp (heaped)	Onion seeds
Pinch	Ginger
	Juice of 1 lemon

Simmer onion in oil until transparent. Add all ingredients, except flour. Bring to boil, reduce heat and simmer for 10 mins Mix flour with a little water to make a thick paste. Gradually stir into sauce and boil for further 5 mins, stirring constantly. Discard bay leaf. For smooth sauce, put in blender for a few seconds.

BASIC SAUCE WITHOUT MILK

Mix 3 level teasp potato flour with 1 tblsp water to thick paste. Gradually add ½ to ¾ pt (1¼-2 cups - 300-450ml) water. Boil for 3 mins, stirring constantly.

For SWEET SAUCE, add Fructose to taste
For SAVORY SAUCE, add vegetable juice instead of water
For WHITE SAUCE, use half water and half soya milk

SALAD DRESSING

1 tin	Soya cream (6 oz)	(¼ cup - 69ml)
	Salt and pepper to taste	
	Herbs to taste	

Pour cream into bowl, discard the whey. Mix salt, pepper and any herbs carefully. Suggested herbs are chopped parsley or chives.

MIXED VEGETABLE JUICE

Although any vegetables may be used a good basic combination is:

12	Tomatoes	
1 each	Onion, lettuce, watercress (bunch), parsley, red pepper and celery	
1 lb each of	Carrots, spinach	(450g)
	Salt & pepper to taste	
1 teasp	Basil	

Wash all vegetables thoroughly, chop and put in large casserole covered with water (except spinach, which boil on its own in a little water). Cover casserole and bake for about 2 hours at 100° electric, 200°F Gas Mark 1. until vegetables are soft. Put in liquidiser with spinach or put through sieve, scraping pulp off with a spoon. This should now be thick, like a purée. To every pint add ½ pint (1¼ cups - 300ml) water and salt, pepper, basil to taste. Bring to boil, reduce heat and simmer for 15 mins. Cool, put in containers, cover and freeze until needed. Otherwise use at once

ICE CREAM

½ pt	Hot water (1 ¼ cups - 300ml)
2 teasp	Gelozone or Agar-Agar (gelatine)
2 tblsp	Fructose (powdered)
1 tin	Soya cream (6 oz) (¼ cup - 69ml)
2 teasp	Vanilla extract
1 tblsp	Walnuts (chopped) [optional]

Gradually blend water and gelatine until smooth. Whisk or blend with Fructose. Add soya cream and vanilla, mix well, put into coldest part of refrigerator until nearly set Remove and whisk well. Return to refrigerator, leave until nearly set again and repeat the blending. This stops the ice cream crystallising. Place in freezer and serve in usual way.

CAROB ICE CREAM
As above, adding 2 tblsp carob powder.

ORANGE ICE CREAM
As above, leaving out vanilla, adding equal parts of water and pure orange juice. You may need a little more Fructose to taste.

STRAWBERRY ICE CREAM
As above, leaving out vanilla, adding 8 oz (2 cups - 225g) strawberries (chopped). Put ¼ pt (12 cup - 150ml) water into pan with strawberries. Cover, bring to boil. reduce heat, simmer until soft and mushy. Cool and strain out pips. Return liquid juice to pan with further ¼ pt water. Add Fructose and simmer until this has melted and liquid is like purée. Blend with cream and proceed as for plain ice cream.
Any kind of chopped nuts, cherries or chopped fruit may be added to the basic ice cream.

MUSHROOM SAUCE

½ pt   Vegetable juice   (1 ¼ cups - 300ml)
2   Mushrooms (chopped) (½ cup -50g)
1 clove   Garlic (peeled & crushed)
1 teasp Potato flour
1 tblsp Sunflower oil
         Salt & pepper to taste

Lightly brown mushroom in oil. Add rest of ingredients, except flour. Bring to boil, reduce heat and simmer for 5 mins. Mix flour with a little water to make paste. Gradually stir paste into stock, boil for further 5 mins, stirring constantly to prevent burning.

PEANUT BUTTER

Grind unsalted peanuts in coffee grinder until they become fine - about 2/3 mins. Blend with margarine to a smooth consistency. Season with salt to taste. This may be frozen for future use, otherwise eat at once.

PEPPER SAUCE

2 tblsp Sunflower oil
2   Red peppers (washed, deseeded & chopped)
         Large onion (peeled & chopped)
1 14oz Tin of tomatoes   (2 cups - 400g)
1 tblsp Tomato purée (home-made)(see page 75)
2 tblsp Water
1 teasp Mixed herbs
½ teasp Paprika
1 tblsp Potato flour
Pinch   Cayenne pepper
         Bay leaf
         Salt & pepper to taste

Simmer onion in oil until lightly brown. Put all ingredients, except flour, in saucepan. Bring to boil, then simmer for 5 mins. Mix flour and a little water, combining to make thick paste. Slowly stir into pan and simmer for further 5 mins. Remove bay leaf.

RAISIN SAUCE

10 oz	Water	(1¼ cups - 300ml)
2 oz	Fructose	(4 tblsp - 50g)
2 oz	Seedless raisins (washed)	(¼ cup - 50g)
2 teasp	Mustard seeds	
1 tblsp	Potato flour	
3 tblsp	Lemon juice	
½ teasp	Margarine	

Put raisins in pan with water, bring to boil, reduce heat and simmer for 10 mins. Put all other ingredients, except flour in pan and simmer for further 15 mins. Mix flour and little water to make paste and stir into sauce. Simmer for further 5 mins.

ROSE HIP SYRUP

2 lb	Rose hips	(900g)
	Fructose	

Cover hips with water, bring to boil and simmer with lid on, until liquid has halved. Cool and strain pulp and liquid through jelly bag or muslin. Reserve liquid and return pulp to pan. Cover with water and reboil until half liquid remains. Cool and strain into previous liquid. For every pint (2½ cups - 600ml) of liquid add 1 lb (400g - 2 cups) Fructose. Reboil in clean saucepan until reduced to thick syrupy consistency. Cool, pour into small containers, cover and freeze for future use.

This keeps for about a week defrosted.

SOYA COTTAGE CHEESE [REPLACEMENT]

1 tin   Soya milk (14 oz)   (2 cups - 400ml)
           Salt & pepper to taste
1 tblsp Lemon juice
           Herbs, such as chopped chives or cayenne
           pepper

Empty milk into shallow dish. Add 1 tblsp lemon juice and stir with wooden spoon. Leave to set for 3 hours, covered with muslin. Then pour into saucepan, bring to boil, reduce heat and add a little more juice. It should then separate: discard the whey. Cool and pour through muslin into bowl, leaving to hang for 2 hours or so. It should then be quite dry, though moist to the touch. Add condiments to taste and herbs of your choice.

TAPIOCA GEL

Put 1 tblsp tapioca into fireproof dish. Pour over about 1 pt (2½ cups - 600ml) boiling water. Put in oven and bake for 30 mins.
150° electric   300°F Gas Mark 2   Centre
This will resemble glue! Pour into containers and freeze for future use; otherwise use immediately. This will be used for macaroons and crackers and can be used in place of egg white.

TOMATO PURÉE

	Ripe tomatoes (chopped)
2	Bay leaves
Pinch	Basil, cayenne pepper
Sprig	Mint
Small bunch	Parsley
	Salt to taste
	Fructose

Put tomatoes and bay leaves in casserole, cover with water and bake for about 2 hours.
150° electric   300°F Gas Mark 2
Take from oven, discard bay leaves, leave to cool. Put through sieve. To every pint of purée, add salt to taste and ½ teasp Fructose. Pour into pan, bring to boil, add herbs, reduce heat and simmer for 10 mins. Cool and pour into liquidiser for a couple of seconds. Put in containers, cover and freeze for future use: otherwise

WESTERN BARBECUE SAUCE

2 teasp	Mustard seeds
4 oz	Haricot beans (soaked overnight) (1 cup - 100g)
1 tblsp	Tomato purée
1 tblsp	Sunflower oil
1 tblsp	Red pepper (washed, deseeded & chopped)
1	Onion (peeled & chopped)
Pinch	Cayenne, oregano, rosemary
	Salt & pepper to taste

Put beans in pan with fresh water, bring to boil, reduce heat and simmer for 15 mins. Add rest of ingredients, except onion. Lightly brown onion in oil in pan, add to sauce, simmer for further 5 mins. Cool and either sieve or put through liquidiser for a couple of mins.

MEDITERRANEAN SAUCE

4 oz	Mushrooms (sliced) (1 cup - 125g)
1	Large onion (peeled & chopped)
1 clove	Garlic (peeled & crushed)
3 tblsp	Tomato purée
	Bay leaf
2 tblsp	Sunflower oil
¾ pt	Mixed vegetable juice (2 cups - 450ml)
1 teasp	Oregano
½ teasp	Dried basil
1 tblsp	Potato flour
16	Black olives (stoned & sliced)
14 oz	Tin of tomatoes (depipped) (2 cups - 425ml)
	Salt & pepper to taste

Lightly fry onion in oil until tender and golden brown, add mushrooms and simmer for 2 mins. Add other ingredients, except flour and olives. Bring to boil, reduce heat and simmer for 20 mins. Mix flour in a little water to thick paste, stir into sauce, add olives, bring to boil and stir until thick (about 3 mins). Remove bay leaf.

PASTRY No. 1

1½ oz	Margarine	(1½ tblsp - 50g)
1½ oz	Sunflower oil	(1½ tblsp - 50ml)
9 oz	Plain flour	(2½ cups - 250g)
Little	Water	

Sift flour into bowl, stir in oil, mix well. Blend in margarine until mixture is crumbly. Lastly add water to make stiff dough. Roll out only once. Use in usual way for pies, tarts, etc.

PASTRY No. 2

6 oz	Plain flour	(1½ cups - 150g)
3 oz	Margarine	(⅓ cup - 75g)
1½ teasp	Pectin	
Little	Water	

Sift flour and pectin, then add margarine. Blend with fork until crumbly. Add water and mix to stiff dough. Roll out gently on lightly floured board. Cover and cool in 'fridge until wanted or freeze for future use.

See also page 38 for alternate pastry in recipe for 'Spinach Crêpe'.

HOT AND COLD DESSERTS

CANADIAN RAISIN PIE

8 oz   Raisins or sultanas   (1½ cups - 225g)
1 tblsp Lemon juice or 1 teasp Vanilla
1 tblsp Fructose
1 teasp Potato flour
          Pastry No. 1 [see page 76]

Wash fruit and cover with water in saucepan. Bring to boil, reduce heat, add Fructose and simmer until fruit resembles grapes in size. Add lemon juice or vanilla. Mix potato flour in a little cold water, then add to fruit, stirring all the time to stop lumps forming. Simmer gently until mixture becomes transparent. Leave to cool. Oil 7 inch pie dish, line with pastry. Pour in fruit. Cover with more pastry. Bake 1 hour.

      200° electric   400° F Gas Mark 6   Centre

CRYSTAL WHIP

Whatever flavour required, add ½ teasp extra of that flavour. This recipe is for strawberry.

½ pt   Boiling strained strawberry juice (1¼ cups - 300ml)
4 tblsp   Gelatine Agar-Agar or Gelozone
½ teasp   Strawberry vegetable flavouring
2 tblsp   Fructose (powdered)
6 oz tin   Soya cream   (½ cup - 169ml)
A few strawberries or nuts for garnishing

Dissolve gelatine in boiling juice, then cool. Place in 'fridge until nearly set, then add cream and flavouring. Beat until frothy. Add Fructose and whisk again until thick. Put in glass dishes and place in 'fridge to set. Garnish.

CRUNCHY PUMPKIN PIE

6 oz   Sweet biscuits [see page 89] (1½ cups - 175g)
4 oz   Margarine (melted)

Crush biscuits finely in coffee grinder. Mix in margarine with a fork. Line a 7 inch pie dish with tin foil and grease. Press biscuit mixture all round bottom and sides of dish. Place in refrigerator to harden before adding pumpkin.

6 oz   Pumpkin (skinned, pips & pulp removed)(175g)
3 oz   Fructose   (6 tblsp - 75g)
¼ teasp Salt
½ teasp Cinnamon
½ teasp Ginger
1 teasp Potato flour
¼ lb   Marzipan [see page 94]
2½ oz   Soya milk   (3 tblsp - 75g)
2½ oz   Water

Boil pumpkin in a little water until cooked. Squeeze all water from it, leaving it quite dry. Return pumpkin to saucepan on a low heat. Add Fructose. Slowly bring to boil and simmer for 5 mins. Add spices and salt. Mix potato flour with milk and water and add to mixture. Bring to boil for 3 mins. Cool. Remove pie shell from refrigerator and spread pumpkin in it. Roll out marzipan on a lightly floured board and cut into ½ inch strips. Lay these over pumpkin to form lattice design. Bake in oven 10-15 mins.

200° electric   400°F Gas Mark 6   Near top

FRUIT PIE

4 oz	Margarine	(½ cup - 100g)
8 oz	Sweet biscuits [see page 89]	(2 cups - 225g)
8 oz	Fructose (powdered)	
1 5 oz	Fruit (pre-cooked with Fructose to taste and thickened with potato flour)	(425g)
1 tblsp heaped	Crushed almonds	
½ pt	Soya cream	(1 cup - 425ml)

Melt margarine and stir into biscuits that have been crushed in blender or with a rolling pin. Well oil a 10 inch pie dish, press biscuit mixture on bottom and round sides of dish. Place in refrigerator until set hard, remove and pour in fruit filling. Top with soya cream, sweetened with enough crushed Fructose to taste. Squeeze rosettes round top of pie and sprinkle with crushed almonds. Leave to set in refrigerator.

FRUIT SALAD

1	Eating apple (peeled, cored & finely chopped)
1	Orange (peeled, depipped & cut in small pieces)
1	Banana (cut into sections)
3	Small peaches (destoned & cut into slices)
¼ pt	Pineapple or orange juice
1 teasp	Lemon juice
Handful white and black grapes (pips removed)	
Handful Cherries (stones removed)	
	Fructose to taste

Put ingredients, except banana, in a large glass dish. Cover with Fructose. The banana should be added just before serving as it is inclined to turn brown. Serve with soya cream.

LEMON CURD PIE

4 oz Pastry No. 1 [see page 76]   (100g)
4 tblsp Lemon curd [see page 93] or enough to cover
       7 inch pie dish
1 tin Soya cream
3 teasp Potato flour

Roll out pastry on floured board. Line pie dish with foil, grease well. Lay pastry over and prick with fork. Bake until golden brown.
    200° electric   400°F Gas Mark 6   Near top
When pastry is cool spread lemon curd. Empty soya cream into either fireproof dish or enamel saucepan. Put this in boiling water over stove and stir in flour (adding extra if not thick enough) constantly to stop lumps forming - 3 mins. Remove from heat. Cool, and pipe cream round top. Place under grill and brown slightly, being careful not to burn. Cool and serve.

MAPLE LEAF DUMPLINGS

4   Medium cooking apples (peeled & cored)
½ teasp Cinnamon
¼ teasp Nutmeg
4 tblsp Maple syrup
6 tblsp Fructose
8 oz   Plain flour   (2 cups - 225g)
4 oz   Margarine   (½ cup - 100g)

Mix sifted flour, margarine and enough water to make stiff dough. Roll out to about ½ inch thick. Cut rounds large enough to cover apples. Mix syrup, Fructose and spices together. Put each apple in pastry circle and pour enough syrup to fill each core hole. Join the circle up on top of each apple, wrap in foil. Put apple dumplings in pan of hot water and bake in oven for 1 hour.

200° electric   400°F Gas Mark 6   Centre

Pour remaining syrup over apples when cooked. Serve
with soya cream.

MAPLE SYRUP PANCAKES

6 oz	Self raising flour	(1½ cups - 175g)
2 oz	Margarine	(¼ cup - 50g)

Mix to stiff dough and roll out to an eighth of an inch.
Cut into 4 inch circles. Fry 5/7 mins in hot oil. Turn
over. Serve with Fructose and lemon or maple syrup.

PANCAKE CHIPS

Any pieces of dough left over cut into strips and fry in
oil. Roll in powdered Fructose and dip into cinnamon
or maple syrup.

SAVORY CHIPS

As above, but sprinkled with paprika.

SAGO, RICE or TAPIOCA PUDDING

½ pt Equal parts soya milk & water (1 cup - 300ml)
1 oz   Fructose   (2 tblsp - 25g)
1 oz   Sago, rice or tapioca   (1 tblsp - 25g)
½ teasp Vanilla extract
I tblsp Margarine
Pinch   Grated nutmeg

Wash grain. Put into fireproof dish with Fructose. Pour
over soya milk. Dot margarine over top and sprinkle
with nutmeg. Bake for ¾ hour.

150° electric 300°F Gas Mark 2 Just above centre
Serve with stewed fruit or cream.
1 tblsp Sultanas may be added to make a change.

SPICED CARROT PUDDING

2½ oz	Carrot (grated)	(½ cup - 75g)
2½ oz	Potato (cooked & mashed)	
2½ oz	Sultanas	
2½ oz	Currants	
2 oz	Breadcrumbs (home-made)	(½ cup - 50g)
2 oz	Self raising flour	
4 oz	Fructose	(½ cup - 100g)
4 oz	Margarine	
1 tblsp	Soya milk	
¼ teasp	Bicarbonate of soda	
½ teasp	Cream of tartar	
½ teasp	Cinnamon	
½ teasp	Mixed spice	
½ teasp	Salt	
1 teasp	Pectin	

Mix margarine and Fructose, add potato and stir well.
Add fruit and carrot and stir again. Then mix in bread
crumbs and flour, pectin, spices, salt and cream of
tartar. Lastly, warm milk to hand heat and stir in
bicarbonate of soda. Add to cake and mix well again.
Turn into well greased bowl large enough for rising.
Cover loosely with foil. Tie edges with string. Put in
large saucepan with water halfway up the side of the
bowl. Bring to boil and turn down heat slightly, but
don't let water go off the boil. Boil for 2 hours. Serve
with soya cream or sauce.

SPONGE FRUIT FLAN

2 oz	Self raising flour	(½ cup - 50g)
2 oz	Fructose	(¼ cup - 50g)
1 teasp	Cider vinegar	
1 teasp	Vanilla extract	
1 teasp	Baking powder	
2 tblsp	Soya milk	
16 oz tin	Peaches or similar sliced fruit	(3 cups - 450g)

Sift flour and baking powder into bowl, add Fructose and milk and beat well. Grease 7 inch flan tin. Pour mixture in and spread evenly. Bake for 20 mins.

190° electric   375° F Gas Mark 5   Near top
When cool remove flan from pan and fill with fruit. Put into refrigerator until set. Serve with soya cream or cream icing.

STEAMED MAPLE PUDDING

3 oz	Breadcrumbs (home-made)	(1 cup - 75g)
3 oz	Self raising flour	(¾ cup - 75g)
3 oz	Margarine	(⅓ cup - 75g)
5 oz	Maple syrup	(½ cup - 150g)
1 teasp	Baking powder	
¼ teasp	Bicarbonate of soda	
1 tblsp	Warm water	

Mix breadcrumbs and flour (sifted with baking powder). Crumble in margarine with fork. Dissolve bicarbonate of soda with water warmed to hand heat, add to crumble mix. Oil a bowl, big enough to allow pudding to rise, and pour syrup into bottom, smooth mixture over top. Cover with foil and tie down with string. Put into saucepan with boiling water halfway up bowl. Cover with lid. Boil gently for 1½ hours. Serve

with a little more warmed syrup or soya cream.
VARIATIONS:

GINGER PUDDING

Add
1 oz	Preserved ginger	(25g)
1 teasp	Ground ginger	
	Omit syrup.	

FRUIT PUDDING

2 oz	Sultanas	(50g)
1 teasp	Mixed spice	

LEMON OR ORANGE PUDDING

Grated rind and juice of large lemon or half an orange.

BREADS AND BISCUITS

BISCUIT DOUGH

6 oz	Plain flour	(1½ cups - 175g)
1½ oz	Margarine	(2 tblsp - 40g)
¼ pt	Soya milk & water	(⅔ cup - 150ml)
Pinch	Salt, mustard seeds	

Sift flour and salt into bowl, add mustard. Rub in margarine. Stir in milk and water with knife until dough is stiff. Roll out on floured board. Cut into 1½ inch rounds. Cook for 15-20 mins.

200° electric 400°F Gas Mark 6 Near top

These rounds may be added to savory casseroles or baked fruit dishes (omitting mustard).

CRACKERS

4 oz	Plain flour	(1 cup - 100g)
2 teasp	Tapioca gel [see page 74]	
2 teasp	Pectin	
1 teasp (heaped)	Margarine	
	Little water to make soft dough	

Sift dry ingredients. Cut margarine into mixture with knife until it resembles breadcrumbs, then add gel and water to make into soft dough. Roll out on floured board to ½ inch thick: cut into 2½ inch squares. Put on baking sheet and prick all over with fork. Bake about 15 mins or until fairly crisp.

200° electric 425°F Gas Mark 7 Near top

Cool on wire tray. Can be made in batches and stored in freezer. Must be cooled right through before storing.

GINGERBREAD

5 oz	Soya milk & water	(⅔ cup - 150ml)
7 oz	Self raising flour	(1¾ cups - 200g)
4 oz	Margarine	(½ cup - 100g)
4 oz	Maple syrup	(½ cup - 100 ml)
2 oz	Fructose	(¼ cup - 50g)
1½ teasp	Bicarbonate of soda	
½ teasp	Salt	
2 teasp	Ground ginger	
¼ teasp	Ground cloves	
1 teasp	Cider vinegar	
1 teasp	Lemon juice	

Sift dry ingredients, except bicarbonate: add vinegar, syrup and juice and mix well. Stir in water gradually. Warm soya milk to hand heat, dissolve bicarbonate of soda and blend into mixture. Pour into well oiled 7 inch cake tin and bake for 1 hour, 20 mins.

190° electric 375°F Gas Mark 5   Just above centre Cool on wire tray. Spread glacé icing over top and dot with crystallised ginger.

MACAROONS

6 oz	Ground almonds	(¾ cup - 175g)
8 oz	Fructose	(1 cup - 225g)
1 teasp	Tapioca gel [see page 74]	
	Glacé cherries	
	Rice paper	

Mix almonds and Fructose with gel to make stiff dough. Oil about 10 bun tins and line bottoms with rice paper. Roll up dough into balls about the size of a large marble. Put on rice paper and press ½ cherry into each ball. Preheat oven and cook for 15 mins, until light gold colour.

120° electric   250°F Gas Mark 2   Centre

PEANUT BUTTER BREAD

8 oz   Plain flour   (2 cups - 225g)
9 oz   Peanut butter [see page 72] (¾ cup - 250g)
3 teasp Baking powder
6 oz   Soya milk   (½ cup - 175ml)
½ teasp Salt

Sift dry ingredients in bowl. Stir in peanut butter. Mix in milk to soft dough. Put in 1 lb (450g) oiled loaf tin and bake for 1 hour.

180° electric   350°F Gas Mark 4   Centre

QUICK LOAF

8 oz   Plain flour   (2 cups - 225g)
1½ oz   Margarine   (1½ tblsp)
5 oz   Soya milk   (⅔ cup - 150ml)
3 teasp   Baking powder
1 tblsp   Fructose
½ teasp   Salt

Sift dry ingredients into bowl. Add margarine which has been melted and cooled. Stir in until mixture resembles crumbs. Add soya milk and mix to stiff dough. Put into greased 1 lb (450g) bread tin. Bake about 1 hour.

190° electric   375°F Gas Mark 5   Centre

PINEAPPLE BREAD

6½ oz	Self raising flour	(1½ cups - 200g)
3½ oz	Margarine	(⅓ Cup - 88g)
3½ oz	Fructose	
2 oz	Crystallised fruit (finely chopped)(¼ cup - 50g)	
1½ teasp	Baking powder	
½ teasp	Mixed spice	
½ teasp	Cinnamon	
¼ teasp	Cream of tartar	
¼ teasp	Bicarbonate of soda	
1½ teasp	Cider vinegar	
1 tblsp	Soya milk	
	Juice & grated rind of ½ lemon	

Sift dry ingredients, except bicarbonate. Cream margarine and Fructose. Bend into flour and mix well. Add juice, rind and vinegar. Warm milk to hand heat and dissolve bicarbonate. Fold into mixture until creamy. Scoop into well oiled 8 inch loaf tin, lined with foil. Bake 1 hour.

SWEET BISCUITS

2 oz	Rice flour	(½ cup - 50g)
2 oz	Sago flour	
1 oz	Margarine	(1 tblsp- 25g)
1 oz	Fructose	
1 tblsp	Soya milk	
½ teasp	Pectin	
½ teasp	Baking powder	
Few drops	Vanilla extract	

Sift dry ingredients. Rub in margarine until it resembles breadcrumbs. Add essence and milk and mix to stiff dough. Roll out on floured board to ¼ inch thick. Cut into 2 inch shapes. Arrange on well oiled baking tray and bake for 10 mins.

220° electric   425°F Gas Mark 7   Near top

SPICED BISCUITS

½ teasp Ginger or cinnamon, plus sultanas for top of each biscuit

CAROB BISCUITS

Remove 1 tblsp flour from basic recipe and replace with 1 tblsp carob powder

Any of these biscuits can be sandwiched with soya cream or apple jelly [see page 68].

CROUTONS

Slices of home-made bread
Remove crusts from bread and slice into 1 inch cubes. Heat oil and brown on all sides. Remove from pan and cool.

ICINGS

ICING SUGAR

To make icing sugar grind Fructose in a blender or coffee grinder for a few seconds.

ALTERNATIVE ICING

8 oz	Fructose	(1 cup - 225g)
1 ½ tblsp	Water	
2 drops	Glycerine (obtained from Chemist)	
Few drops	Vanilla extract or ½ teasp Lemon juice	

Powder Fructose in coffee grinder. Pour into bowl, add water, stir until smooth, add glycerine and flavouring until creamy. This is good for Christmas cakes as it does not harden

BASIC ICING

8 oz	Fructose	(1 cup - 225g)
4 oz	Margarine	(½ cup - 100g)

Few drops Vanilla extract
Powder Fructose in grinder. Empty into bowl and blend in margarine. Add extract and mix well.

CAROB ICING

As above, substituting 1-2 tblsp Carob powder for vanilla and add 1 tblsp water. Mix until smooth.

COFFEE ICING

As above, using 1 teasp Hag or Dandelion coffee substitute, instead of vanilla.

PLAIN CREAM ICING

8 oz	Fructose (powdered in blender)	(1 cup - 225g)
2 oz	Margarine	(¼ Cup - 60g)
Few drops Vanilla extract		

Powder Fructose, blend in margarine. Add vanilla and mix well. If you want icing without margarine, use 2 tblsp cream in its place.

GLAZE

3 tblsp	Fructose
1 tblsp	Water

Powder Fructose in blender, mix with water and pour over cake.

CRYSTALLISED or CANDIED FRUIT

2 lb	Fructose	(4 cups - 900g)
4 tblsp	Fruit juice	

Peel and slice fruit (if using oranges break into sections). The smaller the portions the better. Put fruit in sauce pan, just cover with water and bring to boil, reduce heat and simmer until fruit is just half-cooked. Remove fruit and dry out on paper kitchen towel.
To prepare glaze: Put Fructose and juice in saucepan. Bring to boil to 'crack' stage 290°F. To test this take a little on a spoon and drop it into cold water: if it sets hard at once, the

syrup is ready. Take off heat. Using a toothpick or wooden cocktail stick, spike each piece of fruit and dip it in the syrup. Twirl it round and lay fruit on oiled foil to set, sprinkling with powdered Fructose. Repeat process until all syrup is used. Cool fruit and let it harden. Wrap in small containers or foil, freeze for future use.

Note: almost any fruit is suitable, but be careful to candy only one fruit at a time or flavours will be masked.

MOCHA ICING

6 oz	Fructose	(¾ cup - 175g)
2 oz	Carob powder	(½ cup - 50g)
2 tblsp	Water	
1 teasp	Hag or Dandelion coffee substitute	

Powder Fructose and put in bowl. Add carob powder and mix well. Stir in coffee and water, blend in Fructose. Stir until creamy.

ORANGE or LEMON ICING

Substitute fruit juice for flavouring and add grated zest of fruit.

LEMON CURD

10 oz	Boiling water	(1 cup - 300ml)
4 oz	Fructose	(½ cup - 100g)
4 tblsp (heaped)	Potato flour	
	Large lemon	

Mix flour and juice to fine paste, stir into boiling water with rind of lemon. Stir constantly until mixture thickens. Add Fructose, stir well until dissolved and boil gently for 5 mins. This may be frozen until required, otherwise use immediately.

MARZIPAN

8 oz	Ground almonds	(2½ cups - 225g)
4 oz	Fructose	(½ cup - 100g)
4 oz	Fructose (powdered in blender)	
Little	Soya milk	(½ cup - 100g)

Knead all ingredients together and roll out to required length.
This makes enough for two cakes 6 x 7 inches.

WHIPPED CREAM

2 tblsp	Soya cream
1 teasp	Potato flour or rice flour
	Powdered Fructose to taste

Have ready a large pan of boiling water. Into either an
enamel saucepan or a fireproof dish, mix flour and cream
with a wooden spoon (if metal comes into contact with this
cream it will blacken). Stir until smooth and creamy. Put dish
into boiling water stirring constantly to stop lumps forming:
it takes about 3 mins to thicken. Remove from heat and
continue to stir until cool. Add icing sugar and stir until
smooth. When the mixture has cooled it can be piped on to
puddings, pies or cakes in the normal way.

CAKES

ALMOND FRUIT SQUARES

8 oz	Pastry No. 1 [see page 76]	(225g)
4 oz	Apple pulp	(1 cup - 100g)
3 oz	Currants	(½ cup - 75g)
3 oz	Sultanas or raisins	
1 teasp	Vanilla extract	
4 oz	Marzipan [see page 94]	(l00g)

Line well oiled 11 inch Swiss roll tin with ¾ of the pastry. Cover with mixed apple pulp and vanilla, currants and sultanas. Roll out marzipan and lay half inch strips over the top. Roll out rest of pastry into ¼ inch strips and crisscross over top of marzipan. Bake for 15 mins.

      200° electric   400°F Gas Mark 6   Top

Turn down for a further 15 mins to

      180° electric   350°F Gas Mark 4   Top

BON PARTI CAKE

5 oz	Self raising flour	(1⅓ cups - 150g)
4 oz	Margarine	(½ cup - 100g)
3 oz	Fructose	(⅓ cup - 75g)
½ teasp	Cider vinegar	
½ teasp	Bicarbonate of soda	
¼ teasp	Cream of tartar	
2 tblsp	Carob powder	
1 lb	Marzipan [see page 94]	(450g)
1 tblsp	Soya milk	
1 teasp	Vanilla extract	

Cream margarine and Fructose. Sift flour and cream of tartar, gradually blending with margarine and vinegar. Warm milk to hand heat and dissolve bicarbonate of soda. Add to mixture and beat until creamy. Divide mixture in half. Add carob powder to one half and vanilla to the other. Oil a 7 inch bread tin and line with foil. Place a piece of foil down centre of tin to divide the cake mixtures. Pour plain mixture in one half and carob flavour in the other. Cover with foil and bake for 50 mins or until done.

190° electric   375°F Gas Mark 5   Just above
centre

To test if ready: insert toothpick - if it comes out clean the cake is done.

MARZIPAN COVERING:

Cool cake and trim edge. Cut in half and sandwich together with apple jelly. Cut cake so that colours alternate. Cover sides with apple jelly. Roll out marzipan into large rectangle. wrap this around cake. Seal with apple jelly. Score the top of cake with a fork. Decorate with crystallised fruits [see page 92].

BUTTERFLY CAKES WITH ORANGE ICING

3 oz	Self raising flour	(¾ cup - 75g)
2½ oz	Fructose	(⅓ cup - 75g)
1½ oz	Margarine	(3 tblsp - 38g)
¼ teasp	Bicarbonate of soda	
½ teasp	Cider vinegar	
1 tblsp	Soya milk	
1 dessertspoon	Orange juice and grated rind of small orange	
Pinch	Cream of tartar	

Sift all dry ingredients, except bicarbonate, into bowl.

Melt margarine, add Fructose, cool and scoop into flour gradually. Add vinegar, juice and rind. Warm milk to hand heat. Dissolve bicarbonate of soda in milk and add to batter. Mix well until smooth and creamy. Grease small bun tins. Scoop mixture into each, three quarters of the way up the sides. Bake for 18 mins.

190° electric 375°F Gas Mark 5 Near top
When cool, slice top off each cake. Cut the section in half. Make enough 'basic icing' [see page 91] to pipe rosettes over top of each cake. Stand the two halves on top of cake at an angle to resemble wings, rounded edge outwards. Pipe a little more icing round outside to keep slices upright.

CANADIAN DATE SQUARES

8 oz	Plain flour	(2 cups - 225g)
4 oz	Margarine	(½ cup - 100g)
4 oz	Fructose	
4 oz	Sweet biscuits (crumbled)	(1 cup - 100g)
4 oz	Stoned dates	(½ cup - 100g)
2 oz	Mixed chopped nuts	(½ cup - 75g)
¼ pt	Water	(½ cup - 150ml)
½ teasp	Bicarbonate of soda	

Put water, dates, 2 oz Fructose in saucepan. Bring to boil until thick (about 5 mins), cool. Rub margarine and flour until it resembles crumbs. Add rest of Fructose, biscuit crumbs and bicarbonate of soda. Stir until all ingredients, except date mixture are blended. Oil 8 inch square tin. Spread half cake mixture over tin bottom. Spread date mixture evenly over this, then scoop rest of mixture over dates. Bake for 30/40 mins.

180° electric 350°F Gas Mark 4 Near top
When cool cut into squares. These are better the next day and improve with keeping.

CARAWAY SEED CAKE

6 oz	Self raising flour	(1½ cups - 175g)
3 oz	Fructose	(½ cup - 75g)
3 oz	Margarine	
2 teasp	Cider vinegar	
1 teasp	Baking powder	
¼ teasp	Cream of tartar	
½ teasp	Bicarbonate of soda	
5 oz Equal parts Soya milk & water		(⅔ cup - 150ml)
3 teasp	Caraway seeds	

Sift all dry ingredients, except bicarbonate of soda, into bowl. Melt margarine to hand heat, add Fructose and beat well. Add vinegar and most of soya milk and water, except for 1 tblsp, and beat well. Warm rest of milk and water to hand heat, add bicarbonate of soda, beat into mixture until batter is smooth and creamy. Scoop into 8 x 5 inch loaf tin (oiled and lined with foil). Bake for about 1 hour.

     150° electric   300°F Gas Mark 2   Centre

CAROB CUP CAKE

3½ oz	Self raising flour	(¾ cup - 88g)
2 oz	Margarine	(¼ cup - 50g)
2 oz	Fructose	
½ teasp	Bicarbonate of soda	
¼ teasp	Baking powder	
½ teasp	Cider vinegar	
1 tblsp	Carob powder	
2 tblsp	Water	
2 tblsp	Soya milk	

Sift flour, baking powder and carob powder. Cream margarine and Fructose. Add vinegar and stir until smooth. Then add vanilla. Lastly, mix bicarbonate of soda with milk and water. Mix all together and beat until smooth. Bake in well oiled bun tins for 25 mins.

180° electric 350°F Gas Mark 4 Near top

This recipe makes 6 small cakes. When cool spread with apple jelly [see page 68]. Ice with carob icing [see page 91]. Cover with nuts. Top with a cherry.

CAROB GÂTEAU

2½ oz	Margarine	(⅓ cup - 50g)
3¾ oz	Fructose	(⅔ cup - 100g)
5 oz	Soya milk	(⅔ cup - 150ml)
5 oz	Plain flour	(1½ cups - 150g)
7 tblsp	Carob powder	
2½ teasp	Baking powder	
¼ teasp	Salt	
½ teasp	Vanilla extract	
2 teasp	Cider vinegar	
¼ teasp	Bicarbonate of soda	
½ teasp	Cream of tartar	

Cream margarine and Fructose. Sift all dry ingredients and blend in gradually with margarine. Add vanilla and vinegar. Warm milk to hand heat and dissolve bicarbonate of soda. Pour into cake mixture slowly, stirring all the time. Beat well. Oil and line an 8 inch cake tin. Scoop mixture in evenly and bake for 55-60 mins.

190° electric 375°F Gas Mark 5 Just above centre

Cool on wire tray. Ice with carob icing [see page 91]. Slice cake in half and spread carob icing inside, sound sides and on top. Decorate with glacé lemon slices [see page 92].

CAROB LAYER CAKE

3 oz	Self raising flour	(¾ cup - 75g)
4 oz	Margarine	(½ cup - 100g)
3 oz	Fructose	(⅓ cup - 75g)
1 tblsp	Carob powder	
1 teasp	Apple pectin	
1 teasp	Cider vinegar	
1 teasp	Vanilla essence	
2 tblsp	Soya milk	
2 tblsp	Water	
Pinch	Salt	
	Toasted almonds	

Sift flour, pectin, salt and carob powder. Melt margarine to hand heat and add Fructose. Mix ingredients well until smooth, add vanilla, vinegar, milk and water. Beat until creamy and smooth. Spread mixture in oiled Swiss roll tin, lined with foil or greaseproof paper. Bake for 25 mins.

200° electric   400°F Gas Mark 6   Near top

Ice with either carob or coffee icing [see pages 91 or 92]. Decorate top with toasted almonds.

CHERRY AND WALNUT GÂTEAU

8 oz	Sweet biscuit (crushed)	(2 cups - 225g)
8 oz	Margarine	(1 cup - 225g)
2 oz	Walnuts (chopped)	(½ cup - 50g)
5 oz	Self raising flour	(1¼ cups - 150g)
4 oz	Fructose	(½ cup - 100g)
2 teasp	Cider vinegar	
1 teasp	Almond essence	
1 teasp	Baking powder	
¼ teasp	Cream of tartar	
½ teasp	Bicarbonate of soda	

| 2 tblsp | Soya milk & Water |
| Handful | Cherries (cooked & mashed) |

Oil 10 inch pie dish, line with foil. Mix half margarine and biscuits together and press on bottom and sides of dish. Just cover cherries in water in saucepan, bring to boil, reduce heat and simmer for 10 mins or until liquid has been reduced to half. Sweeten with Fructose to taste, mash and spread mixture in dish. Place in cold compartment of refrigerator for about 2 hours or until set. Cream rest of margarine and Fructose. Sift flour, baking powder and cream of tartar and gradually add margarine. Warm milk to hand heat, mix with bicarbonate of soda, stir into mixture, add rest of ingredients and mix well. Remove pie dish from refrigerator, spread cake mix over evenly. Cover with foil and bake for 70 mins or until done.

200° electric 400°F Gas Mark 6 Just above centre

Cool in dish. Ice with basic icing [page 91], pipe rosettes round edge. Top with walnut halves.

COCONUT LEMON CHIFFON LAYER CAKE

3 oz	Coconut (shredded)	(1 cup - 75g)
2½ oz	Margarine	(3 cup - 50g)
3¾ oz	Fructose	(½ cup - 100g)
5 oz	Soya milk	(⅔ cup - 150ml)
6½ oz	Self raising flour	(1⅔ cups -188g)
2½ teasp	Baking powder	
¼ teasp	Salt	
1 tblsp	Lemon juice & grated zest of lemon	
2 teasp	Cider vinegar	
½ teasp	Bicarbonate of soda	
¼ teasp	Cream of tartar	

Cream margarine and Fructose. Sift flour, salt, cream

of tartar and baking powder and blend into margarine. Stir in vinegar and lemon juice and mix well. Warm milk and water to hand heat and dissolve bicarbonate of soda. Pour into mixture and blend well. Stir in 2 oz coconut (save rest for decoration). Oil and line 8 inch cake tin and spoon mixture over evenly. Bake 1 hour.
190° electric 375°F Gas Mark 5 Just above centre
Slice in two halves (or bake another identical cake). Spread lemon curd [page 93] in centre. Cover with basic icing [page 91], adding a little grated lemon peel. Top with candied lemon slices [page 92] and coconut.

COFFEE FUDGE CAKE

8 oz	Self raising flour	(2 cups - 225g)
3 tblsp	Fructose	
2 tblsp	Margarine	
5 oz	Soya milk	(⅔ cup - 150ml)
1 teasp	Bicarbonate of soda	
1 teasp	Hag or Dandelion coffee	
1 teasp	Vanilla extract	
1 teasp	Cider vinegar	
½ teasp	Salt	

Sift flour and salt. Cream margarine and Fructose, then add flour. Add milk, vanilla, coffee, vinegar and, lastly, bicarbonate of soda added to a little of the milk and warmed to hand heat. Beat well. Line 8 inch tin, grease and scoop mixture in. Bake for 50 mins.
180° electric 350°F Gas Mark 4 Just above centre
Remove from tin and cool on wire tray. Decorate with carob icing [page 91] and walnuts.

CRUNCHY JAM SANDWICH

| 8 oz | Sweet biscuits (crushed) | (2 cups - 225g) |
| 4 oz | Margarine | (½ cup - 100g) |

Melt margarine, mix with biscuit. Press round bottom and sides of 7 inch pie dish. Put in refrigerator until hard.

FILLING

4 oz	Stale cake crumbs	(2 cups - 100g)
4 oz	Marzipan	(½ cup - 100g)
4 tblsp	Apple jelly	
1 oz	Glacé pineapple	

Spread jelly over pie shell, sprinkle with cake crumbs. Roll out marzipan on a little potato flour, cut into ½ inch strips to lay over crumbs. Bake for 20 mins.
190° electric   375° F Gas Mark 5   Near top
When cool, pipe with soya cream and sprinkle top with pieces of glacé pineapple.

DOLCE FRUTTA

8 oz	Self raising flour	(2 cups - 225g)
4 oz	Margarine	(½ cup - 100g)
4 oz	Fructose	
2 oz	Currants	(¼ cup - 50g)
2 oz	Sultanas	
2 oz	Cherries (chopped)	
4 pt	Rooibosch tea (cold)	(⅔ cup- 150ml)
¼ teasp	Salt	
¼ teasp	Cream of tartar	
½ teasp	Bicarbonate of soda	
1 tblsp	Maple syrup	
1 tblsp	Orange or lemon rind	

Put margarine, Fructose, fruit, tea and syrup in pan
and boil for 5 mins. Cool. Add cream of tartar, rind
and sifted flour. Sprinkle in salt, stir until creamy.
Then add bicarbonate of soda and mix well. Scoop into
5 inch cake tin. Bake for 1 hour, 10 mins.
          180° electric 350°F Gas Mark 4   Centre
Remove from oven, leave to cool in tin, then turn on
to wire tray.

FAIRY CUP CAKES

4 oz	Self raising flour	(1 cup - 100g)
2 oz	Fructose	(¼ cup - 50g)
2 oz	Margarine	
1 teasp	Vanilla extract, Hag or dandelion coffee	
1 teasp	Cider vinegar	
1 teasp	Baking powder	
1 tblsp	Soya milk	
2 tblsp	Water	

Sift flour and baking powder. Cream margarine and
Fructose. Add vinegar, flavourings, milk and water.
Add mixture to flour, mix thoroughly until creamy.
Bake in well oiled bun tins for 15 mins.
          190° electric   375°F Gas Mark 5   Near top
Ice with your favourite icing and decorate with walnuts
or cherries.

FROSTED APRICOT AND ALMOND LAYER
CAKE

2 oz	Margarine	(¼ cup - 50g)
3 oz	Fructose	(⅓ cup - 100g)
5 oz	Soya milk & water	(⅔ cup - 150ml)
6 oz	Self raising flour	(1½ cups - 175g)

2½ teasp	Baking powder
¼ teasp	Salt
½ teasp	Almond essence
2 oz	Cider vinegar
½ teasp	Bicarbonate of soda
¼ teasp	Cream of tartar
2 oz	Dried apricots (cooked & sweetened or fresh)

Cream margarine and Fructose. Sift all dry ingredients, except bicarbonate of soda, blend with margarine. Add essence and vinegar and mix well. Warm milk and water to hand heat, dissolve bicarbonate of soda and pour into cake mixture gradually, stirring well. Oil and line 8 inch cake tin, scoop mixture in evenly and bake for 55-60 mins.

190° electric 375°F Gas Mark 6   Just above centre Cool on wire tray. Slice in half or cook similar sized cake. Chop apricots finely and mix with basic icing [page 91] to spread in centre of cake and on sides and top. Decorate with rosettes piped round top and crystallised apricot pieces [page 92].

LEMON OR ORANGE LAYER CAKE

4 oz	Self raising flour	(1 cup - 100g)
2 oz	Margarine	(¼ cup - 50g)
2 oz	Fructose	
1 teasp	Cider vinegar	
½ teasp	Bicarbonate of soda	
1 tblsp	Juice and rind of either orange or lemon	
2 tblsp	Soya milk	
Pinch	Salt	

Sift flour and salt into bowl. Melt margarine and add Fructose. Cool, and pour into flour and mix well. Add juice, finely grated rind and vinegar. Stir well. Lastly, warm. soya milk to hand heat, dissolve bicarbonate of soda in it and add to mixture. Cream well. Scoop into 7 inch cake tin, greased and lined with foil. Cover top and bake for 20 mins.

190° electric 375° F Gas Mark 5 Just above centre

Cool on wire tray. Slice in half or bake a similarly sized cake. Spread lemon curd [see page 93] in centre over top and sides. Ice top and sides in lemon or orange basic icing [page 91], swirl icing round in peaks. Add a few halves of walnuts and glacé fruits as decoration.

LEFT OVER CAKE DELIGHT

	Left over or stale cake
	Left over or stale cake
1 lb	Any kind of fruit (cut into small pieces)
	(3 cups - 450g)
1 tblsp	Pineapple juice
1 tblsp	Margarine
	Fructose to taste

Oil fireproof dish. Put fruit on bottom. Pour on enough water to just cover bottom of dish. Sprinkle on Fructose to taste. Add juice, lastly cover with crumbled cake. Dot all over with margarine. Bake for 30 mins.

200° electric   400°F Gas Mark 6   Near top

MOCHA GÂTEAU

2 oz	Margarine	(¼ cup - 50g)
3 oz	Self raising flour	(¾ cup - 75g)
1 oz	Carob powder	(¼ cup - 25g)
2 oz	Fructose	(¼ cup - 50g)
1 teasp	Hag or Dandelion coffee	
1 teasp	Cider vinegar	

1½ tblsp	Soya milk
1½ tblsp	Water
Few drops	Vanilla extract
Pinch	Salt
Pinch	Cream of tartar
¼ teasp	Bicarbonate of soda

Sift flour, carob powder, cream of tartar and salt. Melt margarine to hand heat, add Fructose, mix and beat well. Add coffee, vanilla and vinegar. Mix bicarbonate of soda with milk and water at hand heat. Blend all ingredients until creamy and smooth. Spread into oiled and lined Swiss roll tin. Bake for about 25 mins.

190° electric 375°F Gas Mark 5 Near top
When cool cut into 4, spread each square with apple jelly. Then add basic icing [page 91], stacking the pieces on top of each other. Ice top and sides. Top with chopped hazel nuts.

MIXED FRUIT CAKE

3 oz	Raisins	(½ cup - 75g)
1½ oz	Currants (floured)	(¼ cup - 38g)
1½ oz	Candied peel	
2 oz	Margarine	(¼ cup - 50g)
3¾ oz	Fructose	(½ cup - 100g)
5 oz	Soya milk and water	(⅔ cup - 150g)
6 oz	Plain flour	(1½ cups - 175g)
2½ teasp	Baking powder	
¼ teasp	Salt	
½ teasp	Almond essence	
2 teasp	Cider vinegar	
¼ teasp	Bicarbonate of soda	
½ teasp	Cream of tartar	

Sift all dry ingredients, except bicarbonate. Cream

margarine, add Fructose, essence, fruit and vinegar. Warm milk and water to hand heat, add bicarbonate. Blend all ingredients until smooth and creamy. Scoop into oiled and lined 8 inch tin. Bake for 55 mins or until done.

190° electric   375°F Gas Mark 5   Just above centre

PARMAPLE CAKE

10 oz	Self raising flour	(2½ cups - 275g)
6 oz	Sesame seeds (finely ground)	(1½ cups - 175g)
3 oz	Fructose	(⅓ cup - 100g)
3 oz	Margarine	(⅓ Cup - 75g)
3 oz	Sunflower oil	(½ cup - 75g)
8 oz	Maple syrup	(¾ cup - 220g)
¼ teasp	Cream of tartar	
½ teasp	Bicarbonate of soda	
1 teasp	Cider vinegar	
1 teasp	Baking powder	
3 oz	Soya milk & water	(¼ cup - 75g)
1 teasp	Ground ginger	
Pinch	Salt	

Sift all dry ingredients, except bicarbonate. Rub in oil and Fructose. Add warmed maple syrup. Warm milk and water to hand heat and add bicarbonate of soda. Stir into dry ingredients. Spread into oiled and lined 8 inch tin. Bake for 1¼ hours.

150° electric   300°F Gas Mark 2   Just above centre

PINEAPPLE CANDY CAKE

4 oz	Self raising flour	(1 cup - 100g)
2 oz	Margarine	(¼ cup - 50g)
2 oz	Fructose	
1 oz	Crystallised fruit (finely chopped) (1 tblsp - 25g)	
½ teasp	Bicarbonate of soda	
1 teasp	Pectin	
½ teasp	Baking powder	
2 tblsp	Rooibosch tea (cold)	
1 tblsp	Water	
Few drops	Almond essence	
Pinch	Salt	
	Apple jelly or pineapple jam	

Mix flour, baking powder and salt. Add fruit. Melt margarine, cool and add Fructose, essence and pectin. Stir well. Warm strained tea and water to hand heat, mix in bicarbonate of soda, pour into mixture and beat until smooth. Oil and line a 7 x 3 bread tin. Bake for 1 hour. Cool on wire tray before icing.

150° electric 300°F Gas Mark 2 Just above centre
Use basic icing, adding finely chopped crystallised pineapple [page 92]. Slice cake in half, spreading apple jelly over lower half. Put top piece over and spread icing over top and sides. Dot small pieces of pineapple over top of finished cake.

PRUNELLA GÂTEAU

7½ oz	Fructose	(1 cup - 200g)
6 oz	Self raising flour	(1½ cups - 175g)
3 oz	Prunes (stoned)	(½ cup - 75g)
¼ pt	Sunflower oil	(⅔ cup - 150ml)
¼ pt	Prune juice	

3 tblsp	Soya milk and water	
2 teasp	Baking powder	
1 teasp	Cinnamon	
1 teasp	Mixed spice	
¼ teasp	Salt	
2 teasp	Cider vinegar	
2 teasp	Vanilla extract	
Little	Apple jelly [page 68]	
	Walnuts (chopped) for icing	

Sift flour and spices, mix in oil and Fructose, except 3 tblsp (reserved for prunes). Put prunes in saucepan with Fructose and a little water; bring to boil, reduce heat and simmer for 10 mins. Strain off juice, mash prunes. Put rest of ingredients together and mix well. Oil 9 inch bread tin. Spoon in mixture and bake for 1 hour, 40 mins.
180° electric 375°F Gas Mark 5 Just above centre
When cool, slice in half and spread with apple jelly. Make cream icing. with enough prune juice to make icing spread. Also add any prune pulp left over. Cover top and sides of cake and sprinkle with nuts.

RAINBOW CELEBRATION CAKE

2½ oz	Margarine	(⅓ cup - 50g)
2½ oz	Fructose	
5 oz	Soya milk & water	(⅔ cup - 150g)
6 oz	Self raising flour	(1½ cups - 175g)
2½ teasp	Baking powder	
½ teasp	Vanilla extract	
2 teasp	Pectin	
¼ teasp	Bicarbonate of soda	
½ teasp	Cream of tartar	
Pinch	Salt	
Little	Apple jelly [page 68]	

Sift flour, salt, cream of tartar and baking powder into bowl. Cream margarine and Fructose, gradually add dry ingredients and mix well. Stir in essence and pectin and add most of soya milk and water, saving a little to bring to hand heat, mixing in bicarbonate of soda. Pour into mixture and beat until bubbly. Scoop mixture into oiled and lined 8 inch cake tin. Cover and bake for 55-60 mins. Cool on wire tray.

190° electric   375° F Gas Mark 5   Just above
centre

For a really grand occasion, make 2 or more cakes and layer them. To get the rainbow effect make a carob flavour cake, top it with a strawberry or raspberry flavour cake. For simple cake, slice in half, spread apple jelly over both sides, fill with carob or coffee replacement icing and spread basic icing [page 91] over top, flavoured with natural juices and grated rind of either orange or lemon. Pipe shells round base of cake, swirls round top, and decorate with home-made crystallised fruit [page 92].

RICH FRUIT CAKE

4 oz	Margarine	(½ cup - 100g)
4 oz	Fructose	
10 oz	Self raising flour	(2½ cups - 275g)
3 oz	Currants	(½ cup - 75g)
3 oz	Sultanas	
3 oz	Cherries (destoned)	
1 oz	Chopped nuts	(¼ cup - 25g)
1 oz	Carrot (finely grated)	
1 tblsp	Maple syrup	
½ teasp	Almond essence	
½ pt	Rooibosch tea (cold & strained)	
1 teasp	Bicarbonate of soda	
½ teasp	Mixed spice	

1 level teasp   Cinnamon
Pinch   Salt

Put tea, carrot, margarine, fruit and syrup in saucepan. Stir until margarine has melted, dissolve Fructose. Boil for 5 mins. Cool and add essence. Sift dry ingredients, except bicarbonate, into bowl. Gradually add cooled fruit mixture and nuts, last adding bicarbonate of soda, dissolved in tea. Blend in gently and pour into 8 inch square tin, oiled and lined with foil. Bake for 90 mins. 180° electric 350°F Gas Mark 5   Just above centre This is a good substitute for Christmas cake, with marzipan and alternative icing [see pages 94 and 91]. Or, almonds can be dotted all over the cake before baking.

ROCKY MOUNTAIN PINWHEELS

8 oz	Plain flour	(2 cups - 225g)
1 oz	Fructose	(2 tblsp - 25g)
1½ oz	Margarine	(3 tblsp- 38g)
5 oz	Soya milk & water	(⅔ cups - 150ml)
4 level teasp	Baking powder	
Pinch	Salt	

Sift dry ingredients into bowl, rub in margarine until crumbly. Stir in Fructose. Add soya milk and water until dough is stiff. Roll out on floured board to ¼ inch thick and about 12 x 10 inches

FILLING:

2 lb	Apple or pear pulp	(2 cups - 900ml)
5 oz	Marzipan [see page 94l	(225g)
1 tblsp	Sultanas	
1 teasp	Cinnamon	
4 oz	Left over cake	(2 cups - 100g)

Roll out marzipan on lightly floured board to about 10 x 8 inches. Lay this on dough. Spread fruit pulp evenly. Sprinkle sultanas and cake crumbs over evenly. Roll up dough to tube shape, sealing edges with little water. Cut into ¾ inch rounds and stand these, cut side up, on a well oiled dish. Sprinkle with cinnamon. Bake for 15 mins. When cool, glaze with icing.

200° electric   400°F Gas Mark 6   Near top

GLAZE:

3 tblsp	Fructose (powdered)
1 tblsp	Hot water

Mix together, cool and pour over pinwheels. To powder Fructose: place in coffee grinder for a few mins, when Fructose will resemble icing sugar.

SPECIAL EASTER CAKE

3½ oz	Fructose (powdered)	(⅓ cup - 100g)
7 oz	Self raising flour	(1¾ cups- 200g)
3½ oz	Margarine	(½ cup - 100g)
4 oz	Candied peel	(¾ cup - 100g)
4 oz	Currants	
1 oz	Ground almonds	(1 tblsp - 25g)
2 teasp	Cider vinegar	
½ teasp	Mixed spice	
½ teasp	Cinnamon	
¼ teasp	Cream of tartar	
½ teasp	Bicarbonate of soda	
1 lb	Marzipan	(4 cups - 450g)
Little	Soya milk	
	Grated rind & juice of ½ lemon	

Sift flour and spices into bowl. Melt margarine and add Fructose. Cool, add to flour and mix well. Add rind and juice, vinegar, cream of tartar, fruit and almonds.

Mix bicarbonate of soda in soya milk and water warmed to hand heat, add to mixture and beat until smooth and creamy. Pour half of mixture into 7 inch round cake tin, oiled and lined with foil. Roll out marzipan and cut two rounds same size as cake tin. Lay one round on mixture in tin, pour balance on top. Bake for 2 hours.

160° electric 375°F Gas Mark 4 Centre

Cool on wire tray. Put second round of marzipan on top of cake. Make round balls of marzipan, put round top of cake and make nest of baby Easter eggs in centre. Decorate with artificial chicks.

SPICED COFFEE CAKE

2 oz	Margarine	(¼ cup - 50g)
3¾ oz	Fructose	(½ cup - 100g)
4 pt	Equal parts soya milk & water (⅔ cup - 150ml)	
6 oz	Self raising f lour (1½ cups - 175g)	
2½ teasp	Baking Powder	
½ teasp	Vanilla extract	
2 teasp	Cider vinegar	
½ teasp	Bicarbonate of soda	
¼ teasp	Cream of tartar	
½ teasp **each**	Cinnamon, Mixed spice, Nutmeg, Cloves	
Pinch	Salt	
	Walnuts for decoration	

Cream margarine and Fructose. Sift all dry ingredients, except bicarbonate. Blend well with margarine; add vinegar and essence. Warm milk and water to hand heat, dissolve bicarbonate and add to mixture. Blend well until creamy and bubbly. Scoop into oiled and lined 8 inch cake tin and bake for 55-60 mins.

190° electric   375°F Gas Mark 5 Just above centre

Cool on wire tray, slice in half and fill with coffee basic icing [see page 91]. Ice edges and top, pipe rosettes on top and decorate with walnuts.

SPICED TEA SQUARES

5 oz	Self raising flour	(1¼ cups - 150g)
2 oz	Margarine	(¼ cup - 50g)
2 oz	Fructose	
1 tblsp	Rooibosch tea	
3 tblsp	Water	
1 teasp	Vanilla extract	
½ teasp	Bicarbonate of soda	
1 teasp	Cider vinegar	
Good pinches	Cinnamon, cream of tartar	

Sift flour, cinnamon and cream of tartar. Melt margarine and add Fructose. Add vanilla, vinegar and some flour to stop curdling. Beat well. Add little cold tea and mix flour in. Add bicarbonate of soda to rest of tea and blend in at hand heat. Beat until smooth. Bake for about 25 m ins .

190° electric   375° F Gas Mark 5   Near top

When cool, spread lemon icing over top. Cut into squares and top with cherries or other decoration of choice.

STRAWBERRY or RASPBERRY SHORTCAKE

8 oz	Plain flour	(2 cups - 225g)
4 oz	Soya milk & water	(½ cup - 100ml)
3 oz	Margarine	(⅓ cup - 75g)
3 teasp	Baking powder	
¼ teasp	Salt	
1 tblsp	Fructose	

Sift flour, salt and baking powder. Cream Fructose and margarine, gradually add flour. Turn out on to floured board. Roll out to ¾ inch thick to fit in 7 inch oiled tin. Put dough in and bake for 15 mins.

 200° electric   400°F Gas Mark 6   Near top
Make a second shortcake in the same way

FILLING:
Mash enough fruit to put between layers, sweeten to taste with Fructose. If wanted spread cream over top and add fruit. Sprinkle with powdered Fructose.

WALNUT COFFEE GÂTEAU

2 oz	Margarine	(¼ cup - 50g)
3¾ oz	Fructose	(½ cup - 100g)
5 oz	Soya milk & water in equal parts	
		(⅔ cups- 150ml)
7 oz	Plain flour	(1½ cups - 200g)
2 oz	Walnuts (fine chopped) (½ cup - 50g)	
2½ teasp	Baking powder	
¼ teasp	Salt	
½ teasp	Vanilla extract	
2 teasp	Pectin	
½ teasp	Bicarbonate of soda	
¼ teasp	Cream of tartar	

Cream margarine and Fructose. Sift dry ingredients and gradually blend with margarine. Add essence. Warm soya milk and water to hand heat and dissolve bicarbonate of soda. Mix with rest of ingredients and stir well. Oil 8 inch cake tin, line with foil and scoop mixture in evenly. Bake for 55-60 mins.

 190° electric 375°F Gas Mark 5 Just above centre
Cool on wire tray. Slice in half. Spread coffee icing [see page 92] over centre, round sides and on top. Pipe

shells or swirls round edge and top with walnut halves.
For a large cake, make a duplicate and place on top.

WALNUT AND COFFEE LAYER CAKE

2½ oz	Margarine	(5 tblsp - 50g)
3¾ oz	Fructose	(⅓ cup - 100g)
5 oz	Soya milk & water	(⅔ cup - 150ml)
7 oz	Plain flour	(1½ cups - 200g)
2 oz	Walnuts (fine chopped)	(½ cup - 50g)
2½ teasp	Baking powder	
½ teasp	Vanilla extract	
2 teasp	Cider vinegar	
½ teasp	Bicarbonate of soda	
¼ teasp	Cream of tartar	
Pinch	Salt	

Sift flour, salt, baking powder and cream of tartar into
bowl. Add Fructose and margarine melted to hand
heat. Cool, add essence. Stir well. Add vinegar,
walnuts, more flour and beat well. Warm soya milk
and water and dissolve bicarbonate of soda. Add to
mixture and beat until smooth and creamy. Scoop into
oiled 8 inch cake tin, lined with foil. Bake for 55 mins.
190° electric 375°F gas Mark 5 Above centre
Cool on wire tray, then slice in half (or bake another
cake similar size). Spread either apricot or apple jelly
[page 68] inside. Spread coffee basic icing [page 91] in
centre and on top and sides. Pipe shells round top
edge. Decorate with walnut halves.

RECIPES FOR CHILDREN

BREAKFAST CEREAL

4 oz   Rice flour   (½ cup - 100g)
4 oz   Potato flour
4 oz   Margarine
4 teasp (level) Baking powder
2 tblsp   Water
2 teasp   Fructose

Sift dry ingredients. Soften margarine over low heat and blend with flour and Fructose until it resembles bread crumbs. Add water and mix well. Put dough on lightly floured board and roll out to about ½ inch thick. Cut into 2½ inch rounds, place on well oiled baking sheet. Bake in oven for 15 mins or until well done.
 230° electric   425°F Gas Mark 7   Just above centre
 Cool on wire tray. Serve biscuits with banana cream or slice in half and spread with margarine. These are suitable for babies as rusks.

HOME-MADE BREAD AND SPICE PUDDING

4 slices   Home-made bread (crusts removed)
2 tblsp   Fructose
Few drops   Vanilla essence
Little   Soya milk

Cut slices into four, spread margarine over each piece. Layer slices on top of each other. Add Fructose. Add vanilla to soya milk and pour over just enough to cover bread. Dot all over with margarine. If liked, sprinkle either nutmeg or cinnamon (for variation add handful of sultanas) between layers of bread. Bake for about 30

mins or until golden brown on top.
190° electric   375°F Gas Mark 5   Centre
This is nice served hot or cold with maple syrup or
fruit purée.

SANDWICH SNACKS

Spread a thin slice of bread with margarine, then with
a small amount of peanut butter [see page 72], sprinkle
alfalfa on top: salt to taste. Cover with second piece of
bread.
Other fillings
Savory soya cream cheese [see page 74]
Tomato (pips removed)
Jam (home-made)
Mashed dates and margarine
Mashed banana
Beetroot & shredded lettuce (washed)
Watercress and mustard & cress
Cucumber, lettuce & soya cream cheese

SOUP FOR YOUNG CHILDREN

3 sticks	Celery (washed & chopped)	
1	Small carrot (scraped & chopped)	
3 tblsp	Spinach (previously cooked)	
1	Small potato (peeled & chopped)	
1 teasp	Split peas	
Pinch	Chives (chopped)	
	Bouquet garni	
1 pt	Water	(2½ cups - 575ml)
	Salt to taste	

Put all ingredients into large saucepan, cover with
water. Bring to boil, then turn down and simmer for ½
hour. Cool. Remove bouquet garni. Put soup through

sieve or blender. Reheat and serve. Any left over can
be frozen when cold (it does not keep out of freezer).

VEGETABLE SOUP

1 pt	Water	(2½ cups - 575ml)
1 bunch	Watercress (thoroughly washed)	
1	Carrot (scraped & chopped)	
1	Small onion (peeled & chopped)	
1 sprig	Parsley (washed)	
2 teasp	Split peas	
1 teasp	Pearl barley	
1 tblsp	Tomato purée	
1 stick	Celery (washed & chopped)	
1	Small potato (peeled & chopped)	
	Bouquet garni	
1 teasp	Curry powder	
	Salt & pepper to taste	

Put all ingredients into saucepan, boil for 30 mins
slowly. Remove bouquet garni. Cool soup and put
through blender or sieve. Reheat and serve.

FRUIT PURÉE

Take one small eating apple or ripe pear. Peel, core
and cut into small pieces. Add ½ sliced banana and
flesh of small orange. Any other fruit is suitable, if it
has no skin or pips - cooked prunes or apricots would
do, for example. Either press fruit through sieve, a
mincer or (better) a blender. This will not keep, so eat
at once or freeze for future occasion.

PARTY TRIFLE

Crumble any left over biscuits into large bowl. Cover with fruit purée to about 1 inch. Dissolve 1 tblsp Agar-Agar or Gelozone in ½ pt fruit juice of any flavour you choose. Pour this over. Place in refrigerator until set. Top with soya cream and sprinkling of ground almonds and with glacé cherries.

Almond fruit squares 95
Alternative icing 91
Apple & onion flan 13
Apple & orange sauce 52
Apple jelly 68
Apricot sauce 51
Asparagus flan 14
Aubergine 14,
Aunt Ethel's speciality 15
Aunt Ethel's spiced supper loaf 16
Avocado pear risotto 17
Banana cream 68
Banana fritters 32
Barbecue sauce 69
Basic icing 91
Basic sauce 69
Bean & potato savory cakes 41
Beans with onion glaze 43
Biscuit dough 86
Boiled beetroot with onion 45
Bon parti cake 95
Bread & spice pudding 118
Breakfast cereal 118
Broad beans with rose hip glaze 44
Broccoli & carrots 46
Brussels sprouts & carrots 46
Brussels sprouts & leeks 47
Butter bean & apricot savour rolls 17
Butter bean paté 11
Butterfly cakes 96
Cabbage & pepper 50
Cabbage envelopes 49
Cabbage fritters 14
Cabbage pancakes 51
Cabbage parcels 21
Cabbage rolls 33
Cabbage slices with onion glaze 48
Canadian date squares 97
Canadian raisin pie 78
Candied fruit 92
Caraway seed cake 98
Carob biscuits 90
Carob cup cake 98
Carob gâteau 99
Carob ice cream 71
Carob icing 91
Carob layer cake 100

Carrot pudding 83
Carrots & broccoli 46
Carrots & Brussels sprouts 46
Carrots & leeks 56
Carrots with haricot beans 43
Casserole of mixed vegetables 52
Cauliflower & chestnut sauce 53
Celeriac with pineapple & sultanas 54
Celery purée 54
Celery soup 9
Celery stuffed with nuts & pineapple 23
Celery stuffed with potato 47
Cheese 74
Cherry & walnut gâteau 100
Chestnut & cauliflower sauce 53
Chinese stir fry 39
Coconut lemon chiffon layer cake 101
Coffee fudge cake 102
Coffee icing 92
Continental quiche 3
Cornish pasty 52
Cottage cheese 74
Cottage pie 23
Country pie 19
Country stir fry 18
Courgettes stuffed with savory prunes 19
Crackers 86
Cream of mushroom soup 9
Cream of vegetable soup 10
Croutons 26,90
Crunchy jam sandwich 103
Crunchy pumpkin pie 79
Crystal whip 78
Crystallised fruit 92
Curried vegetables 20,55
Curry with bananas 40
Dandelion envelopes 55
Date squares 97
Dolce frutta 103
Easter cake 113
Eastern medley 24
Eastern rice 29
Fairy cup cakes 104
Frosted apricot & almond layer cake 104
Fruit pie 80
Fruit pudding 85
Fruit purée 120

Rose hip syrup 73
Runner beans with parsley & garlic 45
Sago pudding 82
Salad dressing 70
Sandwich snacks 119
Sautéed cabbage 50
Savory cabbage rolls 33
Savory chips 82
Savory nut croquets 38
Savory rice cakes 35
Savory rings 37
Savory sauce 69
Savory spinach crêpes 38
Scarlet runner beans 44
Soup for young children 119
Soya cottage cheese 74
Special Easter cake 113
Spice sauce 18
Spiced biscuits 90
Spiced carrot pudding 83
Spiced coffee cake 114
Spiced savory loaf 34
Spiced supper dish 39
Spiced supper loaf 16
Spiced tea squares 115
Spinach & noodles Italiane 64
Spinach & potato cakes 62
Spinach & potato envelopes 30
Spinach & potato gâteau 64
Spinach crêpes 38
Spinach flan 37
Sponge fruit flan 84
Steamed maple pudding 84
Strawberry ice cream 71
Strawberry shortcake 115
Stuffed beetroot 45
Stuffed courgettes 54
Stuffed marrow 25
Stuffed mushrooms 57
Stuffed tomatoes 36,65
Sweet biscuits 89
Sweet potato, raisin & nut pie 35
Sweet sauce 69
Tapioca pudding 82
Tapioca gel 74
Tomato purée 75
Turnip & potato snowballs 61
Vegetable brunch 66

Vegetable cobbler 27
Vegetable pie 66
Vegetable roly-poly 67
Vegetable soup 11,119
Walnut & coffee layer cake 117
Walnut coffee gâteau 116
Western barbecue sauce 26,75
Whipped cream 4,94
White sauce 69